DURCH STARTEN

ENGLISCH

8

TESTBUCH

Verfasserinnen: Sonja Häusler und Katrin Pürer

Diesem Buch ist ein Lösungsheft zu den Übungen beigelegt.

Entspricht der Rechtschreibreform 2006

Bibliografische Information der Deutschen Bibliothek:
Die Deutsche Bibliothek verzeichnet diese Publikation in der Deutschen Nationalbibliografie; detaillierte bibliografische Daten sind im Internet über http://dnb.ddb.de abrufbar.

VERITAS-VERLAG, Linz
www.durchstarten.at

Lektorat: Klaus Kopinitsch
Covergestaltung: Gottfried Moritz
Illustrationen: Helmut »Dino« Breneis
Satz: Anton Froschauer
Herstellung: Julia Dresch

Gedruckt in Österreich auf umweltfreundlich hergestelltem Papier

3. Auflage 2015
ISBN 978-3-7058-8590-5

VERITAS
Gemeinsam besser lernen

INHALTSVERZEICHNIS

EINLEITUNG ... 3

PROGRESS CHECKS ... 5

Progress Check 1: Ireland ... 6
Progress Check 2: Mysteries, crimes and murderers ... 8
Progress Check 3: Growing up – Kids speak out ... 10
Progress Check 4: Beautiful Boston ... 12
Progress Check 5: Jobs ... 14
Progress Check 6: Hungry? ... 16
Progress Check 7: Super heroes ... 18
Progress Check 8: Australia ... 20
Progress Check 9: Your body ... 22
Progress Check 10: Crazy hobbies ... 24
Progress Check 11: Save our world! ... 26
Progress Check 12: Ready, steady ... reading ... 28
Progress Check 13: Outer space ... 30
Progress Check 14: A school mag ... 32
Progress Check 15: Native Americans ... 34
Progress Check 16: New York ... 36

SCHULARBEITEN ... 39

Schularbeit 1 ... 40
Schularbeit 2 ... 44
Schularbeit 3 ... 48
Schularbeit 4 ... 52
Schularbeit 5 ... 56
Schularbeit 6 ... 60
Schularbeit 7 ... 64
Schularbeit 8 ... 68

BILDUNGSSTANDARDS ... 72

Was sind Bildungsstandards? ... 72
Standardisierte Aufgaben zum Bereich Hören ... 74
Standardisierte Aufgaben zum Bereich Lesen ... 82

WRITING ... 90

APPENDIX: THE FINAL CHECK-UP ... 92

EINLEITUNG

4. Klasse – das letzte Jahr in der Unterstufe! Jetzt heißt es noch einmal so richtig „Gas geben", damit du am Ende dieses Schuljahres eine gute Note im Zeugnis stehen hast. Vielleicht wirst du das Zeugnis auch brauchen, um dich an einer anderen Schule vorzustellen und zu bewerben. In jedem Fall ist es ein tolles Gefühl und du wirst zufrieden mit dir sein, wenn du das Jahr gut abschließt, denn gute Noten sind bekanntlich der Beweis für Fleiß, harte Arbeit und gute Leistungen.

Das Englisch Testbuch für die 8. Schulstufe ist hierfür das perfekte Hilfsmittel! Es ist ein völlig neuartiges Buch, welches ausschließlich – wie der Name schon verrät – **Testformate** bietet und es dir so ermöglicht, deinen Wissensstand fortlaufend zu testen, zu kontrollieren und gegebenenfalls zu verbessern.

Wie funktioniert das Testbuch?

Mittels eines vorgegebenen **Punkteschlüssels** kannst du dich selbst ganz einfach beurteilen und dir so deine **Note ausrechnen.** Dadurch weißt du immer genau, wie es um dein Wissen steht und ob du vielleicht den einen oder anderen Grammatikaspekt noch ein wenig genauer anschauen oder vielleicht sogar nachlernen musst. Du fängst also am besten am Anfang des Schuljahres mit den ersten Kapiteln an und arbeitest dich im Laufe des Jahres durch das ganze Buch durch. Thematisch und inhaltlich ist das Testbuch auf die gängigen Schulbücher abgestimmt. Dadurch sollte es dir also leicht fallen, in die hier vorgegebenen Themen einzusteigen.

Wie ist das Testbuch aufgebaut?

Das Buch unterteilt sich in folgende vier Abschnitte:

- **PROGRESS CHECKS**

  ... sind **Lernzielkontrollen** (jeweils **zweiseitig**), welche abwechselnd entweder eine Hör- oder Leseübung bieten sowie Grammatikübungen.

- **TESTS (Schularbeiten)**

  ... sind optimale Übung und Vorbereitung für tatsächliche **Schularbeiten**. Sie sind jeweils **vierseitig** und bestehen aus einer Hörübung, einer Leseübung und zwei bis drei Grammatikübungen.

- **BILDUNGSSTANDARDS**

  Das ist ein Schlagwort, das wohl in Zukunft immer wichtiger werden wird. Bildungsstandards sind einheitlich vorgegebene Testungen (ähnlich wie die Zentralmatura am Ende der Oberstufe) und sollen sicherstellen, dass alle Schüler einer gewissen Schulstufe das gleiche Niveau erreicht haben. Eine nähere Erklärung zu den Bildungsstandards findest du direkt im betreffenden Abschnitt. Dieser bietet dir außerdem die Möglichkeit, Hör- und Leseübungen zu bearbeiten, die bereits diesen **vorgegebenen Testformaten** entsprechen. Vielleicht wirken die Aufgabenstellungen auf den ersten Blick ein wenig befremdend, aber du wirst sehen, es ist alles halb so wild!

- **WRITING**

  In einem Testbuch darf natürlich auch die Textproduktion nicht fehlen, weil das Schreiben eigener Texte und kleiner Geschichten ja auch fester Bestandteil jeder Schularbeit ist. Da es aber kaum möglich ist, deine Geschichten zu bewerten, werden in diesem Abschnitt nur mögliche **Vorschläge für Schreibthemen** gemacht. Du kannst sie als Übung für die Schularbeit bearbeiten, anschließend im **Lösungsheft** unseren Vorschlag für eine mögliche Umsetzung des Themas studieren und dir vielleicht noch Ideen und Anregungen holen.

Zum Schluss möchten wie dir noch ganz viel Erfolg und natürlich auch Spaß beim Absolvieren deines letzten Jahres in der Unterstufe wünschen! Bitte denke daran, dass ein halbes Schuljahr schnell um ist – denn alle unter euch, die sich in einer anderen Schule bewerben wollen, brauchen bereits eine **gute Note im Semesterzeugnis**! Pack das Jahr also an und lass dir vom Englisch Testbuch für die 8. Schulstufe dabei helfen!

Viel Erfolg!

Sonja Häusler & Katrin Pürer

PROGRESS CHECKS

Der erste Teil deines Testbuches soll dir helfen, dir in regelmäßigen Abständen einen Überblick über dein Können zu verschaffen. Schnapp dir also etwa alle zwei Wochen dein Testbuch und überprüfe, was du schon alles kannst und was du noch üben solltest.

ZEITMANAGEMENT

Bei allen Tests ist dein Zeitmanagement von Bedeutung. Für einen Progress Check solltest du nicht mehr als **10 bis 15 Minuten** brauchen. Stoppe die Zeit, die du benötigst, und kontrolliere, ob du das Zeitlimit auch ja nicht überschreitest!

BEURTEILUNG

Jeder Progress Check wird mit **maximal 50 Punkten** beurteilt. Du findest unter jeder Aufgabenstellung einen individuellen Punkteschlüssel. Vergleiche deine Antworten mit den Lösungen im Lösungsheft und rechne dir deine erreichte Punktezahl aus. Dann vergleiche diese mit folgendem Schema:

Punkte	Note
45,5–50	Sehr gut
40,5–45	Gut
33–40	Befriedigend
25–32,5	Genügend
0–24,5	Nicht genügend

Jetzt weißt du, wie es um deinen momentanen Wissensstand steht!

NERVOSITÄT

Merke dir: Ein Test ist eine Möglichkeit, unter Beweis zu stellen, was man schon kann. Jeder Test zeigt dir, worin du gut bist und was du noch ein bisschen genauer üben solltest. Ein Test ist also Wegweiser und Hilfesteller auf dem Weg durch die Schule! Es besteht daher kein Grund, nervös zu sein oder gar Angst zu haben. Nimm dieses Buch als Chance, dich an **Testsituationen** zu **gewöhnen**, deine **Leistungen** zu **steigern** und **Spaß am Besserwerden** zu gewinnen!

Testdauer: 15 min

Progress Check 1: Ireland

Listening: A language course in Dublin

CD-TRACK 01

Task 1: Vocabulary

5 points (1 point each)

Match the words with the definitions. Fill in the matching letters next to the numbers.

1. language course	**A** a bus for tourists	**1**	
2. foreign country	**B** a place worth seeing	**2**	
3. host family	**C** classes where you learn a foreign language	**3**	
4. sight	**D** land different to your native land	**4**	
5. coach	**E** family where you stay during your trip	**5**	

Task 2: True or false?

12 points (2 points each)

1. Katya did a language course in Dublin. ☐
2. Jennifer stayed in Ireland with her family. ☐
3. The host mother cooked things the girl liked. ☐
4. Jennifer had classes from 9 to 12:15. ☐
5. In the evenings, she went out a lot. ☐
6. During her stay, she went on two organised coach trips. ☐

Task 3: Key answers

8 points (2 points each)

1. What does Jennifer say about the teacher?

   ____

2. Why did she not go out to party in the evenings?

   ____

3. What is "Viking Adventure"?

   ____

4. Would Jennifer like to go back to Ireland?

   ____

Grammar: Past continuous/progressive

TIPP

Bildung	Verwendung
was/were + verb-ing *was not / were not + verb-ing* *Was/Were* + Subjekt + *verb-ing*	■ Eine Handlung in der Vergangenheit war im Verlauf. ■ Ein ganz genauer Zeitpunkt in der Vergangenheit wird angegeben.

Task 1: Past continous

Fill in the correct forms of the verbs in brackets in past continuous.

1. While Phoebe ______________________ (*sit*) in the garden,

   Tom ______________________ (*write*) a love letter to her.

2. What ______________________ (*Joe – do*) yesterday at ten?
3. I ______________________ (*not talk*) to Alex when you called me! I swear!
4. ______________________ (*the sun – shine*) when you woke up?
5. We ______________________ (*have*) a lot of fun when you called us.

9 points
(1.5 points each)

Task 2: Past simple or continuous?

Fill in the forms of the verbs in brackets in past simple or continuous.

Last summer, Sophie ____________ (*go*) to Ireland on a language trip. At first, she ____________ (*not be*) very happy because her best friend Nicole ____________ (*not can*) come with her. But finally, Sophie ____________ (*decide*) to enjoy her stay on her own. When Sophie ____________ (*arrive*), her host family ______________________ (*wait*) for her. They ____________ (*welcome*) her and then ____________ (*drive*) her to their house. While Ciara, Sophie's host mum, ______________________ (*take*) her on a tour through the house, Sam, the host dad, ______________________ (*cook*) steak with green beans for the family. They ______________________ (*have*) their dinner, when suddenly Sophie's mobile ____________ (*ring*). It ____________ (*be*) Nicole who ____________ (*tell*) her that she ______________________ (*wait*) outside! Sophie ____________ (*feel*) very happy!

16 points
(1 point each)

Gesamt-
punktezahl

Testdauer:
15 min

Progress Check 2: Mysteries, crimes and murderers

Reading: CSI at school

Task 1: Vocabulary

10 points (2 points each)

Match the words with the definitions and fill in the letters next to the numbers.

1. to search for
2. to discover
3. to return
4. to damage
5. immediately

A to find out; to find somebody/something
B to come back somewhere
C to ruin or destroy something
D at once
E to look for somebody/something

1	
2	
3	
4	
5	

Willford High is a rather small High School outside the center of Wales. It's a private school and nothing has happened there so far. But that's no longer the case because somebody broke into the headmaster's office last Friday night. Mrs Killby, the school's secretary, was the first one who discovered that someting was wrong when she returned to the school on Monday morning. After she had walked into her office, she saw that the door to the headmaster's room was damaged. Mrs Killby immediately called the police and soon three men of the Wales Police Department arrived and started their work. They had brought along a lot of important-looking things which helped them to take finger prints and search for DNA. Mrs Killby was very excited because of their work but the headmaster, in contrast, was not so relaxed because he already knew who had broken into his office. He himself did that when he returned to the school on Friday evening. He had forgotten to take notes with him which he needed for the weekend. As he had left his key at home, he damaged the door. Unfortunately he had not told his secretary and when he arrived on Monday morning, it was already too late. The police had already started their investigation and now the headmaster had to confess what he had done. What a shame!

Task 2: True or false?

16 points (2 points each)

1. On Monday morning Mrs Killby arrived after the headmaster. ☐
2. Somebody had smashed the window of the headmaster's office. ☐
3. Mrs Killby hadn't waited a long time before she called the police. ☐
4. The secretary thought the policemen were exciting. ☐
5. The headmaster felt rather relaxed all the time. ☐
6. Nobody knew who had broken into the office. ☐
7. The headmaster's confession will be a surprise for everybody. ☐
8. It was the headmaster's own fault that all that had happened. ☐

Grammar: Past perfect tense

TIPP

Past perfect	
Bildung	**Verwendung**
had + 3. Form des Verbs … *statement* *had not* + 3. Form des Verbs … *negation* *had* + Subjekt + 3. Form … *question*	Eine Handlung in der Vorvergangenheit – also vor der Vergangenheit; immer nur in Kombination mit der *past tense*

Task 1: Past perfect

Fill in the correct forms of the verbs in brackets in the past perfect tense.

1. Inspector Thackery ____________ (*talk*) to the headmaster and at the same time he ____________ (*read*) through the police file again.
2. ________ the headmaster ____________ (*break*) into his office?
3. Nobody ____________ (*see*) the person who commited the crime.
4. The policemen ____________ (*not ask*) the students.
5. The CSI investigators ____________ (*take*) fingerprints.

9 points (1.5 points each)

Task 2: Past simple or past perfect?

Fill in the forms of the verbs in brackets in past simple or past perfect.

Hi, I'm Jason Reth and I'm a cop. I ____________ (*start*) working for the police after I ____________ (*finish*) school. It's an exciting job as lots of weird things happen. Last Saturday, for example, I ____________ (*be*) on my way home from work. I ________ (*be*) tired because I ____________ (*work*) very hard. My boss ____________ (*call*) me to inform me about a murder that ____________ (*happen*). He ____________ (*tell*) me that a man ____________ (*find*) a dead woman and that she ____________ (*be*) dead for 24 hours. I ____________ (*not be*) happy to hear all that but I ____________ (*must*) go there. In the end it ____________ (*turn*) out that somebody ____________ (*rob*) and ____________ (*stab*) her.

15 points (1 point each)

Gesamtpunktezahl

Progress Check 3: Growing up – Kids speak out

Testdauer: 15 min

Listening: Teenage problems

CD-TRACK 02

Task 1: Who says what?

Fill in: **C** for Cheryl **P** for Phil **F** for Fred **R** for Rita

1. We can't all look perfect, you know. ☐
2. Someone is watching me. ☐
3. I don't want to tell my parents. ☐
4. Don't be embarrassed. ☐
5. My classmates don't want me in my team. ☐
6. My mouth is closed in every picture. ☐
7. You must do something about it. ☐
8. Try to make a joke about yourself. ☐

16 points (2 points each)

Task 2: Multiple choice

Tick the correct ending.

1. Cheryl asks listeners who have a problem
   - **a.** to write her a letter. ☐
   - **b.** to call her. ☐
   - **c.** to send her an e-mail. ☐

2. Cheryl tells Fred
   - **a.** to try whitening toothpaste. ☐
   - **b.** not to smile. ☐
   - **c.** to see the dentist. ☐

3. Rita calls Cheryl because
   - **a.** her parents don't believe her. ☐
   - **b.** she is afraid of her new neighbour. ☐
   - **c.** a strange family has moved in across the road. ☐

9 points (3 points each)

Grammar: Infinitive/Conjunctions

Task 1: Want someone to do something/Infinitive construction

Bildung:	*want/tell/ask* + Person (*object pronoun*) + *to*-Infinitiv

Translate the following sentences. Use to-infinitive constructions.

1. Susan will nicht, dass ich ihre beste Freundin anquatsche. ____________________

____

2. Hat Patrick dir gesagt, dass du ihn in Ruhe lassen sollst? ____________________

____

3. Dein Trainer wird dich vielleicht bitten, mit den anderen Schritt zu halten. ____________

____

4. Mein Vater will nicht, dass ich mit älteren Jungs ausgehe. ____________________

____

5. Gestern hat Ben Tina nicht gefragt, ob sie mit ihm ins Kino gehen will. ______________

____

15 points
(3 points each)

Task 2: Conjunctions

Cause/Result: because of	**Contrast:** Although, However	**Purpose:** so that, in order to

Fill in one of the conjunctions above to complete the sentences.

Dear agony aunt,

I have a big problem. ______________ I am already 14, I am not allowed to stay out longer than nine at weekends. My friends even do not ask me anymore to join them ______________ my early curfew. I have already offered to help mum in the house ______________ make her see that I am a responsible young girl. ______________, she has not yet responded to my offer. What can I do ______________ my parents will finally allow me to stay out longer?

Yours, Sophie

10 points
(2 points each)

Gesamt-
punktezahl

Testdauer:
15 min

Progress Check 4: Beautiful Boston

Reading: My trip to Boston

My name is Elisabeth and I attend Rubbershire Girl's High, which is in the centre of London. I really like my school, the teachers and my classmates but nevertheless I decided to take part in an exchange programme with our partner school in Boston. At first I was very insecure if I should really do that because I was afraid that I would miss my family and my friends. **1**________ What would it be like to live in another city, away from the people and places you know? **2**________ I worried that the students there might not like me or that I don't come along with my host family. What if I turned homesick? **3**________ But then I had long conversations with my parents and they told me that everything would turn out fine and that they were sure I would like it there. **4**________ I was even told about the Salem witch trails, about a thing called "The Boston Tea Party" and lots about sports. So finally I started to feel more comfortable about this whole thing and I decided to really go for it. **5**________ And I have to say that is was one of the best things I have ever experienced in my life. When I came back I told my parents that I had met many nice people and that I had had lots of fun there.

Task 1: Filling in sentences

Put the sentences (A–F) into the gaps (1–5), taking care that there is 1 extra sentence you don't need.

A Would anybody care for me and understand me?
B What would it feel like to be completely alone?
C I also didn't know what to take with me.
D I simply said to myself that it's now or never.
E You have to know that especially my parents are very important for me.
F My dad went to Boston once so he knew lots of interesting stories.

10 points
(2 points each)

Task 2: Sentence completion

1. I like Rubbershire High because ______________________.
2. At first it made me feel ______________________ to think about the trip.
3. My greatest fear was to miss ______________________.
4. ______________________ helped me to find a decision.
5. So afterwards I felt much more ______________________.
6. I must say that my trip to Boston was ______________________.

12 points
(2 points each)

Grammar: Reported (Indirect) speech

TIPP

Reported speech	
Bildung	**Verwendung**
Achtung auf Zeitensprünge, wenn das *reporting verb* in der *past tense* steht!	Um indirekte Rede wiederzugeben (was jemand gesagt hat).

Task 1: Change expressions

DIRECT SPEECH	REPORTED/INDIRECT SPEECH
today	
	the next day/the following day
yesterday	
	that
these	
here	
	then
last week	
	the last year
	the next month

10 points (1 point each)

Task 2: Reported statements

Put the statements into reported speech but take care of the tense of the reporting verb:

1. Sheila said, "I will go to my best friend's place tomorrow." ____________________

____

2. The boys cried, "We are hungry now and want something to eat!" ____________________

____

3. The teacher says, "I will collect your work next week." ____________________

____

4. Billy shouts to his brother, "I took away your favourite toy yesterday." ____________________

____

5. My neighbours said to me, "You have really grown up since last summer." ____________________

____

6. Paula said to Lucy, "You aren't allowed to tell anybody in here." ____________________

____

18 points (3 points each)

Gesamt-punktezahl

Testdauer:
15 min

Progress Check 5: Jobs

Listening: Job application

CD-TRACK 03

Task 1: Sentence completion

Complete the sentences with the missing words.

1. We asked her to tell us about her job ____________________ experience.
2. I did everything to make a ____________ ____________________.
3. She looked a ____________.
4. She has some ____________ coming here.
5. I mean, I was really ____________________.
6. He said something about her diploma and her ___________ at school.
7. She should ____________ to work on Monday.
8. This job ____________ at least a high school diploma.
9. I ____________ ____________ so much into that application.
10. I'll get the ____________________ I need for a good job.

10 points
(1 point each)

Task 2: Which is correct?

Tick the correct sentences.

1. Hal and Katya get a lot of letters from pupils. ☐
2. Leslie had put a lot of effort into her outer appearance for the interview. ☐
3. The applicant in front of her was about 30 years old. ☐
4. At first sight, the other applicant made a good impression on Leslie. ☐
5. When Leslie saw the other applicant, she felt insecure. ☐
6. The other applicant surprised the man with her good education. ☐
7. Leslie thought that she would get the job. ☐
8. Leslie didn't get the job because of her messy style. ☐
9. To get the job, Leslie would have needed a high school diploma. ☐
10. Leslie is now looking for another job. ☐

15 points
(1.5 points each)

Grammar: Reported speech

TIPP

Reported speech – Questions	
Wh-questions *Peter asked, "Where are you?"*	Fragewort + Aussagesatz *Peter asked me where I was.*
Yes/No questions *Peter asked, "Do you love me?"*	*If* + Aussagesatz *Peter asked me if I loved him.*

Task 1: Reported questions

Maggie tells her best friend Mylie about the questions she was asked in her first job interview. Write a text putting the questions into reported speech.

When did you finish school?
Have you already gained any experience in this field?
Will you be prepared to spend some time abroad?
How many languages do you speak?
What are your best qualities?

First, he asked me ______________________________

____

____

____

____

____

10 points
(2 points each)

Task 2: Reported speech

Jenna's first job as a reporter was to interview Johnny Depp. After the interview, she writes an e-mail to her best friend Cora, telling her about it. Read the interview and write that e-mail in reported speech on an extra sheet.

Jenna: *May* I ask you some questions?
Johnny: *Sure*. What do you *want* to know?
Jenna: When *did* you *play* your first role?
Johnny: That *was* in 1984. I *remember* that it *was* in "A nightmare on Elm Street".
Jenna: In how many films *have* you *starred* so far?
Johnny: That *must be* nearly 50 films, as far as I *remember*.
Jenna: *Do* you *have* any favourite film?
Johnny: *I'm not sure*. I *like* all of them.
Jenna: *Thank you* for the interview.
Johnny: It *was* my pleasure.

Start like this: Dear Cora,
Imagine what has happened! I interviewed Johnny Depp! Let me tell you about it. First, ...

15 points
(1 point for each phrase written in *italics*)

Gesamtpunktezahl

Testdauer:
15 min

Progress Check 6: Hungry?

Reading: Jamie Oliver

Task 1: Vocabulary

6 points
(1 point each)

Match the adjectives with the food and fill in the letters next to the numbers.

1. bitter	**A** lemon	**1**	
2. spicy/hot	**B** strawberry, blueberry, raspberry	**2**	
3. sour	**C** muffin, ice-cream, browny	**3**	
4. sweet	**D** chips, crisps	**4**	
5. salty	**E** grapefruit	**5**	
6. fruity	**F** chilli, pepper	**6**	

Ever heard about Jamie Oliver? No, then just go on reading and inform yourself about Jamie Oliver's food philosophy, his work and the importance of eating healthy food. Jamie was born in 1975 and as his father owned a restaurant, he was in touch with the topic of food from the very beginning onwards. But Jamie has gone his own way, becoming enormously popular in the last few years. By now he is not only famous for his TV cooking show but also for his books, his online publications, his DVDs, his restaurants and the products he sells. But what does he actually think about food? For Jamie, food has always been something to enjoy. But lately more people have become fat or even obese and so food has turned into their enemy. They simply don't know what is healthy and unhealthy and what they should eat or, respectively, should not eat. Since the last few years this problem has also become relevant for teenagers and even kids. These days 25% of teenagers are obese, which means that they simply weigh too much. Besides, kids with fat parents are twice as likely to become fat when they are grown up. So, according to Jamie, it's time to start thinking about the quality and the quantity of the food we eat to make sure that we don't end up being too fat.

Task 2: True or false?

18 points
(2 points each)

1. Jamie Oliver is a famous cook. ☐
2. There was no connection to food in Jamie's childhood. ☐
3. Having a healthy diet is not important for Jamie. ☐
4. Being obese means you slightly weigh too much. ☐
5. Jamie's career was the same as his father's. ☐
6. People can buy Jamie Oliver products. ☐
7. Today one quarter of the teenagers are obese. ☐
8. If you have fat parents, you have good chances to stay slim. ☐
9. It's important to think about how much we actually eat. ☐

Grammar: Revision of tenses

Task 1: Tenses

Complete the following text about food with the correct tenses (present simple/progressive, past simple/progressive, present perfect simple, will-/going to-future):

Hi everyone, I'm Simon and I would like to give you my opinion about food! First of all, I really ____________________ (*love*) eating. My favourite dish is my mum's lamb chops with potatoes and green beans … yummy! Usually I __________________ (*do*) a lot of sports so I can eat a lot. But three weeks ago I ____________________ (*break*) my arm while I _________________________ (*play*) soccer so I _________________________ (*have*) a plaster since then. And this _____________________ (*mean*) that I can do far less sports and also eat less. I personally _____________________ (*think*) that these days people ___________________________ (*not care*) enough about what they eat and if they ________________________ (*eat*) the right things. Some time ago this _______________________ (*be*) different, I think. In earlier times people only ______________________ (*eat*) when they ____________________ (*be*) hungry. They __________________________________ (*not eat*) because they ________________ (*feel*) bored. People _______________________ (*be*) also more active and of course they ________________________ (*not go*) by car all the time as it ____________________ (*be*) the case today. I think this phenomenon and tendency _____________________ (*go*) on in the future and people ____ (*even/become*) more lazy than they are right now. I'm sure that the number of obese people _______________________________________ (*increase*) which ____ (*result*) in a growing number of health problems. At the moment, for example, a significant number of teenagers __________________________ (*suffer*) from diabetes while others __________________________ (*have*) a much too high blood pressure. This _______________________ (*must*) change, of course but everybody ______________________ (*know*) that this ____________________ (*be*) difficult.

26 points
(1 point each)

Gesamt-
punktezahl

Testdauer: 15 min

Progress Check 7: Super heroes

Listening: The science that makes Superman so, well, super

CD-TRACK 04

Task 1: Find the numbers.

10 points (2 points each)

1. For how many seasons did the initial words announce Superman? ______________
2. When did Jerry Siegel and Joe Shuster create Superman? ______________
3. At which speed can you jump over a 660 feet high building? ______________
4. What is, according to Prof. Kakalios, the speed of the sound? ______________
5. When did Superman become more and more powerful? ______________

Task 2: Multiple choice

15 points (3 points each)

Tick the correct answer.

1. Who is George Reeves?
   - a. The creator of Superman. ☐
   - b. The first Superman actor. ☐
   - c. The director of the Superman films. ☐
2. Which powers did the original Superman have in 1938?
   - a. He could lift cars and planets. ☐
   - b. He could fly. ☐
   - c. He could jump big distances. ☐
3. Why does Prof. Kakalios say that Superman's hearing is beyond super?
   - a. Because he can hear the crack of a gun from great distances. ☐
   - b. Because he can hear sounds before they have happened. ☐
   - c. Because he can hear the thunder before we see the lightening. ☐
4. Why was, according to Prof. Kakalios, Kryptonite introduced in the 1960s?
   - a. To make the story more interesting. ☐
   - b. To make people aware of the dangers of radioactive power. ☐
   - c. To give the story a scientific touch. ☐
5. Which scientific improvements influenced the comic in the 1930s most?
   - a. Airplanes gave birth to the idea of flying cars. ☐
   - b. Electricity was seen as a source of big power. ☐
   - c. Atomic power inspired science fiction fantasies like jet packs. ☐

Grammar: Adjective or adverb/Question tags

TIPP

Adjective (dangerous)	**Adverb of manner** (dangerous**ly**)
Beschreibt, wie etwas **ist: Hauptwort** *My father is a dangerous **driver**.*	Beschreibt, wie man etwas **tut: Zeitwort** *My father **drives** dangerously.*

Task 1: Adjective or adverb?

1. Come here ____________. Sorry, I'm not so ____________. (*schnell, 2x*)
2. That soup tastes very ____________ (*gut*).
3. My father cooks very ____________ (*gut*).
4. Don't look at me so ____________ (*wütend*).
5. This cake looks ____________ (*köstlich*).
6. Turn the volume up! That song sounds ________________ (*fantastisch*).
7. I'm sorry. I can't hear you ____________ (*gut*).
8. Your girlfriend smiles very ________________ (*schön*).
9. Taste the pie ________________ (*vorsichtig*).

15 points
(1.5 points each)

Question tags	bejahender Satz: verneinend	verneinender Satz: bejahend
Oder? Nicht wahr?	*These muffins are great, **aren't they?***	*This isn't your car, **is it?***

Task 2: Find the correct question tag.

1. You haven't invited Hugh to the party, ______________?
2. Monika cooks very well, ______________?
3. Tim will join us at the club, ______________?
4. Alexandra is on holiday on the Maldives, ______________?
5. Jake didn't forget your birthday, ______________?
6. George has a new girlfriend, ______________?
7. They don't go out much at weekends, ______________?
8. You have got new shoes, ________________?
9. She played in your band last year, ______________?
10. That black cat over there is yours, ______________?

10 points
(1 point each)

Gesamt-
punktezahl

Testdauer:
15 min

Progress Check 8: Australia

Reading: Aborigines

About 22 million people live in Australia, the country "Down Under" as it is often called. 400,000 of these are Aborigines. Until the year 1967 the Australian government made the decisions for the Aborigines. Since that year, Aborigines have officially been citizens of Australia and discrimination has stopped. Or should have stopped, better said. In fact there is still no balance between the lives of Aborigines and that of white people, especially as far as health services and education is concerned. Australia is a rather rich country but nevertheless many Aborigines live a very poor life and don't even have enough money to afford food or a decent apartment. It's common that they live in slums or outside big cities in primitive and simple houses. They also often suffer from diseases but again, they don't have the money to buy medicine as access to medical care is very difficult for them. In addition, Aborigines usually don't have a good education. Because of that they often don't find good jobs and end up becoming criminals in order to finance their lives. It goes without saying that this is a very problematic aspect. Of course the situation slowly gets better but it is still difficult, also for young people. What is more, young Aborigines face the dilemma that they find themselves being in a conflict between living a traditional life and/or a modern life.

Task 1: Vocabulary

8 points (1 point each)

Find the opposites of these words:

to stop	______________	rich	______________
big	______________	to buy	______________
difficult	______________	good	______________
to find	______________	slowly	______________

Task 2: Comprehension

8 points (2 points each)

Answer the questions in full English sentences:

1. Why were the Aborigines not independent before the year 1967? ______________

2. Why are the lives of Aborigines and white people still not equal? ______________

3. Where do poor Aborigines usually live? ______________

4. Why do many Aborigines end up being criminals? ______________

Grammar: Present tense for future meaning

TIPP

Um die Zukunft auszudrücken, verwenden wir:	
PRESENT SIMPLE	**PRESENT PROGRESSIVE**
… wenn wir zB über Programme, Stundenpläne oder Kinozeiten/Zugzeiten usw. sprechen.	… wenn wir über Termine sprechen, die bereits ausgemacht wurden, bzw. Handlungen, die stattfinden werden.

Task 1: Present progressive

Use the words in brackets to write sentences in the present progressive tense:

1. (*write exam/next Monday*) She ______________________________
2. (*leave for Italy/May*) They ______________________________
3. (*meet friends/cinema*) Ryan ______________________________
4. (*play volleyball/evening*) I ______________________________
5. (*buy PSP/for Christmas*) He ______________________________

10 points
(2 points each)

Task 2: Expressing future

Complete the sentences with the words in present simple or progressive:

1. Our neighbours ______________________ (*go*) to the theatre today evening.
2. ______________________________________ (*the concert/start*) at 6:30?
3. We ______________________ (*have*) a big party at the weekend.
4. I __________________________ (*not/go*) on holiday this summer. What a pity.
5. The English lesson _____________________ (*start*) in five minutes.
6. The trains all _____________________ (*leave*) in half an hour from gates 4 and 5.
7. What time ____ (*the next train/arrive*)?
8. ____________________________________ (*you/play*) football with me after school?
9. Alex and Susan ______________________ (*get*) married in June.
10. I _______________________ (*work*) tomorrow afternoon on my English presentation.
11. When ____ (*the film/begin*)?
12. The exhibition (= Ausstellung) ____________________ (*open*) on September 21st.

24 points
(2 points each)

Gesamtpunktezahl

Testdauer:
15 min

Progress Check 9: Your body

Listening: Fitness

CD-TRACK 05

Task 1: Who says what?

Fill in:

N for Nicki **L** for Lizzy **C** for Caroline **J** for Jennifer **P** for Phil

1. I've got a CD with music which helps me relax.
2. I never take the bus or the underground.
3. Next month, I will take part in a competition.
4. I do go to the swimming pool in summer.
5. Swimming trains your muscles.
6. I always wear a helmet.
7. It gives me the energy I need to go through the day.
8. All this talk about fitness is rubbish.
9. Fitness is important to me.
10. I've been in a lot of trouble.

12.5 points
(1.25 points each)

Task 2: True or false?

1. Nicki goes mountain-biking nearly every Sunday.
2. The path behind Nicki's house isn't very difficult.
3. Lizzy went to her first yoga lesson with her friend.
4. Lizzy now practices yoga at home.
5. Caroline often gets stuck in traffic jams.
6. In-line skating is forbidden in Caroline's school.
7. Jennifer goes swimming three times a week.
8. She only swims to stay fit.
9. Phil is sceptical towards fitness.
10. Phil thinks that doing exercise in rain and snow is healthy.

12.5 points
(1.25 points each)

Grammar: Modal verbs

Task 1: Expressing possibility: may/might/could

Rewrite the sentences. Use the words in brackets.

1. Don't forget your umbrella. Perhaps it will rain in the afternoon. (*might*)

   ____

2. Leave your purse in the hotel room. It is possible that you lose it. (*could*)

   ____

3. Ask Troy for help. It's possible that he will help you. (*may*)

   ____

4. Put on your cute skirt! We will possibly meet the boys. (*might*)

   ____

5. Ask her! It's possible that she will invite you to the party too. (*may*)

   ____

6. Don't take my dog off the lead! It's possible that it runs off. (*could*)

   ____

9 points
(1.5 points each)

Task 2: Modal verbs

Fill in the correct modal verbs in the correct tense.
Sometimes, there are two versions possible.

1. Yesterday evening, Alan ________________ (*müssen*) look after his little sister.
2. I'm afraid Trisha ________________ (*nicht dürfen*) see you tomorrow.
3. My daddy ________________ (*nicht können*) repair my bike last weekend.
4. Don't touch this! It ________________ (*könnte*) break!
5. Rick ________________ (*nicht dürfen*) go out without having done his homework.
6. Perhaps Gillian ________________ (*nicht können*) help you next Monday.
7. My cat Sugar ________________ (*müssen*) eat out of her bowl.
8. Last summer, no one ________________ (*nicht dürfen*) swim in the pool.

16 points
(2 points each)

Gesamt-
punktezahl

Testdauer:
15 min

Progress Check 10: Crazy hobbies

Reading: Body piercing

Trisha Wilton is 17 years old, she has long blond hair and blue eyes and from the description so far people would probably say that she is a completely normal teenager. Well, yes she is but something is really special about Trisha: she's got 14 piercings on her body and that's quite a lot. She had her first piercing done when she was 13 and of course it was without her parents' permission. On TV Trisha had seen an actress with a nose piercing and she immediately liked that look. So she decided to have one herself. For sure, when Trisha came home and her mother realised what her daughter had done, there was a big quarrel and Trisha wasn't allowed to go out with friends for a very long time. But in the end her parents got used to their daughter's new look and they had to accept it. However, it didn't take a long time until the next piercings followed and by now Trisha's most striking piercings are her lip and her eyebrow piercings. It's surprising that Trisha has never been afraid of any dangers related to her piercings because there are numerous. Only think about possible allergic reactions or dangerous infections. Anyway, Trisha is happy with the way she looks and she is currently thinking about putting some more metal through her body.

Task 1: Matching sentence halves

At first Trisha's description of her look	she looks different.
But you soon find out	were very angry with her.
Because of these 14 piercings	been afraid of any dangers.
She had her first piercing done	they accepted their daughter's look.
In the beginning her parents	sounds normal and unspectacular.
After some time	some more piercings.
Today Trisha even wants	when she was rather young.
The girl has never	that she has got lots of piercings.

8 points
(1 point each)

Task 2: Error correction

Correct the following sentences so that they are true according to the text:

1. When people look at Trisha they say there's nothing unusual about her.

____

2. Trisha's mother joined her daughter when the first piercing was done.

____

3. After the first piercing years passed before Trisha had her second piercing.

____

6 points
(2 points each)

Grammar: Present perfect or past simple?

TIPP

THE PRESENT PERFECT TENSE	THE PAST SIMPLE TENSE
■ Handlung **nicht** abgeschlossen ■ Verbindung mit der Gegenwart	■ abgeschlossene Handlungen ■ keine Verbindung mit der Gegenwart

Task 1: Spotting signal words

Decide if the following signal words belong to the present perfect tense (PP) or to the past simple tense (PS):

1. lately		**7.** for		**13.** never	
2. last year		**8.** yesterday		**14.** last spring	
3. recently		**9.** ever		**15.** until now	
4. so far		**10.** last weekend		**16.** yet	
5. up to now		**11.** two days ago		**17.** already	
6. in 2009		**12.** since		**18.** just	

18 points (1 point each)

Task 2: Past simple or present perfect?

Fill in the forms of the verbs in brackets in present perfect or past simple:

People have crazy hobbies, mine is climbing. I ______________________ (*do*) that now for 5 years which means that I ______________ (*start*) when I was 22. At that time my friend ______________ (*inspire*) me to try it and I ______________ (*like*) it. And I ______________________ (*love*) doing it since then. Luckily I ______________________ (*never/be*) afraid of accidents even though a friend of mine ______________ (*hurt*) herself last summer. A stone ______________ (*crash*) down, ______________ (*hit*) her and she ______________ (*fall*) down. She ______________ (*wound*) her knee and I'm happy that she ______________ (*not/have*) another accident since then. I ______________________ (*always/train*) hard to avoid falling down and I'm happy nothing ______________________ (*happen*) to me so far. At first my family ______________ (*not/like*) me going climbing but they ______________ (*got*) used to it by now. When I ______________ (*start*) this hobby they ______________ (*not/be*) happy about it of course.

18 points (1 point each)

Gesamt-punktezahl

Testdauer: 15 min

Progress Check 11: Save our world!

Listening: Portland, Oregon, rides the bike

CD-TRACK 06

Task 1: Multiple choice

1. People in Portland use the bike more often these days

- **a.** because it's healthy. ☐
- **b.** because gas prices have increased. ☐
- **c.** because it's better for the environment. ☐

2. Kathleen Schlach reports on

- **a.** a normal working day in Portland. ☐
- **b.** the weather in Portland. ☐
- **c.** a bike race in Portland. ☐

3. How many more percent of bikes cross Hawthorne Bridge than last year?

- **a.** 6 ☐
- **b.** 16 ☐
- **c.** 60 ☐

4. The bike concept of Portland is based on the concept of

- **a.** America. ☐
- **b.** Asia. ☐
- **c.** Europe. ☐

5. Riding the bike in Holland is more popular because

- **a.** bikes are cheaper there. ☐
- **b.** gas is more expensive there. ☐
- **c.** biking is safer there. ☐

15 points (3 points each)

Task 2: Complete the sentences.

1. It's just __________ __________ in Portland.

2. There are four __________ __________, two headed in each direction.

3. In Europe, cycling is safe, ____________________, and the easiest way to get around.

4. Chris Salt __________ __________ maybe three-quarters of the time.

5. __________ in Holland ride in bike lanes completely separated from cars.

10 points (2 points each)

Grammar: Conditional (If-sentences)

TIPP

Conditional 3		
Bedingung: vergangen	**Folge: gegenwärtig**	**Folge: vergangen**
If I had learned more,	*I would know the answer now.*	*I would have known the answer.*
If + past perfect	*would + Nennform*	*would + have + 3rd form*

Task 1: Conditional 3

Complete the sentences with the correct conditional 3-forms.

1. I ______________________ (*call*) you if I ______________ (*have*) the time.
2. If she ______________ (*see*) you she ______________________________ (*invite*) you.
3. My car __________________________________ (*not break down*) if the mechanic ____________________ (*check*) it more carefully.
4. If you ____________________ (*not forget*) to set the alarm, you ____________________ (*not be*) late now.
5. That room ____________________ (*look*) more beautiful if you ______________ (*use*) a brighter colour for the walls.

10 points
(2 points each)

Task 2: Mixed conditionals

Read the example sentences. Then write matching conditional sentences.

1. It is not raining. The sun is shining. I won't take an umbrella with me.

   ____

2. It is hot. You want to go swimming in the afternoon. It is likely to stay hot.

   ____

3. You forget ice-cream in the sun. It melts.

   ____

4. You forgot to call your girlfriend. She is angry now. ____________________

   ____

5. Jeff wrote a bad mark. He was not allowed to go to the cinema yesterday. ______________

   ____

15 points
(3 points each)

Gesamt-
punktezahl

Testdauer: 15 min

Progress Check 12: Ready, steady … reading

Reading: Diary entry

Dear Diary,

I cannot tell you how sad, angry and disappointed I am. You remember Steve, don't you? He's that cute guy from class 4A. Anyway, he's not that good at German and as we've started reading this novel by Christine Nöstlinger, he asked me if I could help him with it. Of course I could! You know how long I had been waiting for a moment like that ☺! So we fixed Friday afternoon for doing the school stuff first and then we wanted to go to the cinema. He said that he would invite me to the new 3D movie and I was really excited. Going to the cinema with Steven – it's like a dream has come true!! However, after we had read the novel and done the exercise (this took us almost three hours), he asked me what time my mum would pick me up. I was surprised and said that she would do so after the cinema. And then he told me that he didn't have time to go to the movie with me because he had already fixed a date with his best friends. They wanted to play pool and then go to a party. I cannot express how angry I was at that moment. Steve had only invited me to read this Nöstlinger stuff with him and I was stupid enough to really think that he wanted to spend time with me. Oh diary, I'm so fed up with boys!

Melanie

Task 1: Find the correct order.

12 points (1.5 points each)

Put the sentences into the correct order to get a summary of the diary entry:

When they started to read a novel, Steve asked Melanie to help him. ☐

But then things developed differently and Melanie was sad and angry. ☐

Melanie couldn't do anything but call her mum to pick her up. ☐

Of course Melanie helped Steve and she felt excited and happy. ☐

Melanie has fallen in love with a guy from her neighbouring class. ☐

Instead of going to the cinema with Melanie, Steve met his friends. ☐

In the end she realised that Steve had only met her for his homework. ☐

He also promised her to invite her to the cinema after she had helped him. ☐

Task 2: True or false?

10 points (2 points each)

1. Melanie is good at German. ☐
2. It was not for a long time that Melanie was keen on meeting Steve. ☐
3. Reading Christine Nöstlinger and doing the exercise were soon over. ☐
4. Steve told Melanie in time that they would not go to the cinema. ☐
5. In the end Melanie thought that she was rather naive. ☐

Grammar: Reflexive pronouns

TIPP

REFLEXIVE PRONOUNS		
Das rückbezügliche Pronomen bezieht sich direkt auf das Subjekt.	*I … myself* *you … yourself* *he … himself* *she … herself* *it … itself*	*we … ourselves* *you … yourselves* *they … themselves*

Task 1: Reflexive pronouns

Fill in a suitable reflexive pronoun:

1. Mum, you needn't help me because I can do it ______________________________.
2. Don't worry, the girls can do their homework ______________________________.
3. Did the cat really open that box all by ___________________________?
4. Usually dad repairs his car ________________________. He can easily do that.
5. Tim and Tony, did you really bake the cake _________________________?
6. We often stick to _________________________. We don't really like other people.
7. Sophie, can you wash the dishes ________________________?
8. The boys bought new trousers for __________________________.
9. The teacher always carries the books __________________________________.

18 points
(2 points each)

Task 2: Mixed pronouns

Fill in any suitable pronoun:

Hello everyone! I'm Mindy and this is what I think about reading:

Well, reading is not exactly ______________ favourite hobby. ____________ sometimes read in my holidays but not very often. ______________ brother is different. ______________ reads whenever he can and he is really keen on books. He buys them ________________ or he borrows ______________ from friends. However, if I read books I do so together with my best friend Caroline. Then _____________ sit down on her bed and get _________________ some cookies and orange juice. Sometimes her mum comes into the room and asks __________________ if we need anything. But usually we are happy with what ______________ have.

10 points
(1 point each)

Gesamt-
punktezahl

Progress Check 13: Outer space

Testdauer: 15 min

Listening: A UFO in Texas?

CD-TRACK 07

Task 1: Key answers

Find the answers to the questions. Do not use more than 4 words.

1. How many people claimed that they had seen a UFO in Stephenville?
   ____
2. To what kind of flying object did the people compare the UFO?
   ____
3. What did the two fighter jets, according to witnesses, do?
   ____
4. How are the Texan people who saw the UFO described by Wade Goodwyn?
   ____
5. Which explanation does the local Air Force give for the UFOs?
   ____

10 points (2 points each)

Task 2: Find the numbers.

1. How many yards was the UFO away from the eyewitnesses? ________
2. For how many minutes was the UFO seen in the air? ________
3. According to the newspaper, how many witnesses were there? ________
4. According to a pilot, the UFO flew faster than ... miles an hour. ________
5. According to that pilot, the UFO was ... mile long. ________

7.5 points (1.5 points each)

Task 3: True or false?

1. The interview is being made in Stephenville, Texas. ☐
2. People saw the UFO only from very far away. ☐
3. Texan people are very down-to-earth kind of people. ☐
4. Alex Cohan does not believe in the UFO theory. ☐
5. There is a lot of evidence proving the existence of that UFO. ☐

7.5 points (1.5 points each)

Grammar: Phrasal verbs

Task 1: Phrasal verbs matching

Match the phrasal verbs with the correct meaning.

1.	turn into	**A**	auf jemanden warten	**1**	
2.	get on with sb.	**B**	aufheben	**2**	
3.	spend on	**C**	losgehen, starten	**3**	
4.	run out of	**D**	ansehen	**4**	
5.	to pick up	**E**	aufpassen	**5**	
6.	wait for sb.	**F**	wegfliegen	**6**	
7.	set off	**G**	sich etwas einfallen lassen, vorschlagen	**7**	
8.	come up with	**H**	wählen aus	**8**	
9.	look at	**I**	ausgeben für	**9**	
10.	blow up	**J**	auseinanderbrechen/sich trennen	**10**	
11.	look after	**K**	mit jemandem auskommen	**11**	
12.	fly off	**L**	abheben	**12**	
13.	choose from	**M**	sich verwandeln in	**13**	
14.	take off	**N**	aufblasen	**14**	
15.	break up	**O**	etwas geht aus, man hat nichts mehr	**15**	

15 points
(1 point each)

Task 2: Translation

Translate the following sentences. Use a phrasal verb.

1. Wie kam der neue Pilot mit der Mannschaft aus?

   ____

2. Was sucht dein Hund da im Garten?

   ____

3. Oh nein! Uns ist die Milch ausgegangen!

   ____

4. Wie viel Geld gibst du nomalerweise für Kleidung aus?

   ____

5. Wirst du morgen auf deine kleine Schwester aufpassen müssen?

   ____

10 points
(2 points each)

Gesamt-
punktezahl

Testdauer: 15 min

Progress Check 14: A school mag

Reading: July in Vienna? ... anything but boring!

I'm Heather. I'm 14 and I live in Boston. Last summer my parents sent me to Austria to spend the holidays there. They also wanted me to learn German and so they organised my stay at an Austrian host family that lived in Lower Austria. The first days were great fun because I got to know my host family better and the area where I stayed. I had a host sister, she was about my age and I really liked her. We stayed up late, slept long, met friends of her or went shopping. But after a few weeks things started to get boring. So she took me with her to discover Austria's capital city Vienna. First of all we went to one of the open air baths which all present big pool areas and playgrounds. It was amazing there. In the afternoon we went to the town hall square and I could hardly believe my eyes. There were uncountable small huts and in every of these huts you could buy food. Food from all over the world, directly cooked in front of you. While we were walking across this square, different smells hit me and made my nostrils feel like being on holiday. First in Greece, then in Turkey and finally in India and Mexico. If I had been able to, I would have stayed there for the rest of the evening. When we went home by train, I was tired and exhaused but also happy.

Task 1: Gap-filling

12 points (2 points each)

Complete this summary with the words given (there are 3 extra words which you don't need!):

highlight – interested – enjoyed – stay – spotlight – arrival – bored – welcome – wish

It was not Heather's ______________ to spend her summer holidays in Austria. Her parents wanted her to do so. After her ________________, she met her host family and she came along with them well. They also had a daughter and she had Heather's age. The two girls did many things together and Heather __________________ her trip. But after some time she felt ________________ so the host daughter took her to Vienna. That was a ________________ for Heather, especially the food court in front of the town hall. She would have even liked to _________________ there longer.

Task 2: Vocabulary matching

8 points (2 points each)

1. host family
2. boring
3. amazing
4. hut

A unbelievable, incredible, fascinating
B a very small house, often made of wood
C not your own family
D not exciting, uninteresting

1	
2	
3	
4	

Grammar: Adverbs

TIPP

Bildung	Verwendung	Einige Ausnahmen
Durch Anhängen von *-ly* an das Adjektiv: *e.g. sad – sadly* *bad – badly* *careful – carefully*	■ Um Verben näher zu beschreiben (wie wird etwas gemacht) ■ Um Adjektive näher zu beschreiben	*fast – fast* *hard – hard* *near – near* *late – late* *fair – fair*

Task 1: Adjective or adverb?

Fill in an adjective or an adverb:

Tim is in class 4B and he works for the school mag. He is a ______________ ______________ (*real/good*) worker because he can do his work very ______________ (*quick*) and ______________ (*easy*). Tim always does a ______________ (*good*) job because when he writes about events at school, he does that ______________ (*careful*). He first makes ______________ (*long*) interviews and he tries to be ______________ (*polite*) and to talk with the people ______________ (*calm*) and ______________ (*friendly*). Normally he smiles at them ______________ (*happy*) and he looks them ______________ (*direct*) into their eyes. Only once he did his job ______________ (*bad*) because he ______________ (*near*) forgot what to ask. On that day he was ______________ ______________ (*real/ excited*) and so this interview was rather ______________ (*hard*) for him. But in the end there was ______________ (*hard*) any need to be nervous any longer. So he kept on working ______________ (*hard*) and wrote an ______________ (*excellent*) article. That interview was ______________ (*fair*) difficult for him but also a ______________ (*good*) training what to do in ______________ ______________ (*real/demanding*) situations like these. Tim is a ______________ (*clever*) boy and working for the school mag is ______________ (*great*) fun for him. Also his ______________ (*good*) friends help him ______________ (*regular*) and sometimes ______________ (*quick*) read through his articles. He's ______________ (*extreme*) thankful for that.

30 points
(1 point each)

Gesamtpunktezahl

Progress Check 15: Native Americans

Testdauer: 15 min

Listening: The story of the eagle

CD-TRACK 08

Task 1: Multiple choice

1. When George Silver Eagle was eight
   - a. his father was very proud of him. ☐
   - b. he felt as if nobody could hurt him on his pony. ☐
   - c. his father taught him to shoot with a gun. ☐

2. The buffalo was important to Silver Eagle's tribe
   - a. because they were holy animals. ☐
   - b. because they needed them to live. ☐
   - c. because they could ride on them. ☐

3. What did Red Feather tell his tribe about the "pale people"?
   - a. That palefaces would take their land and drive the buffalo off. ☐
   - b. That palefaces would try to kill their tribe. ☐
   - c. That palefaces are very sick people. ☐

4. Why did Silver Eagle leave his tribe and go to white men?
   - a. Because Silver Eagle did not like living in Reservation. ☐
   - b. Because his father did not want him to stay with them anymore. ☐
   - c. Because his father wanted him to learn about the white man's traditions. ☐

5. Why was Silver Eagle's hair cut off when he moved in with white people?
   - a. Because white people wanted to educate him to become a white man. ☐
   - b. Because his parents had died. ☐
   - c. Because the white people did not like his long hair. ☐

15 points (3 points each)

Task 2: Complete the sentences.

1. My father taught me to be ______________.
2. The ______________ would run away and take our way of life with them.
3. Women ______________ the meat for food.
4. My father wanted to understand the ______________ of white men.
5. Our own clothes were ______________ ______________.

10 points (2 points each)

Grammar: Passive voice

TIPP	Passive voice		
	"to be" (richtige Zeit!) + 3rd *form of verb*	Aktiv: Passiv:	*My mum cleans my room.* *My room is cleaned by my mum.*

Task 1: Passive voice

Write passive sentences.

1. White people drove Native Americans off their land. ______________________________
2. Many Native Americans have forgotten their stories and traditions. ______________________________
3. The government will help Native Americans to find a job. ______________________________
4. Alcohol and unemployment affect many Native Americans. ______________________________
5. More and more people are teaching children on their native culture. ______________________________

10 points
(2 points each)

Task 2: Passive & tenses

Write passive sentences with the words in brackets. Mind the tenses!

1. Oh no! My purse ______________________________ (*steal*).
2. This bridge ______________________________ (*repair*) at the moment.
3. Last year, I ______________________________ (*not invite*) to your party!
4. I think this room ______________________________ (*clean*) tomorrow.
5. ______________________________ (*the store – filmed*) when the robbery happened?
6. The answer to the quiz question ______________________________ (*not yet – find*).
7. When ______________________________ (*this house – build*)? In 1654.
8. My car ______________________________ (*wash*) every weekend.
9. I hope that squirrel ______________________________ (*not catch*) by our cat.
10. Your last homework ______________________________ (*not do*) properly!

15 points
(1.5 points each)

Gesamt-
punktezahl

Testdauer: 15 min

Progress Check 16: New York

Reading: New York – CSI and Sex and the City

Task 1: Vocabulary

6 points (1 point each)

1. numerous
2. murderer
3. cosmopolitan
4. a bagel
5. a food court
6. to settle

A a person who has killed somebody
B to set up and start a new life somewhere
C a place where you get something to eat
D fascinating, open-minded, attractive
E many, a big number of something
F a soft round bread, very tasty

1	
2	
3	
4	
5	
6	

Who hasn't watched one of the numerous CSI investigation series where murderers are detected and arrested in New York? Or who hasn't followed Carrie (Sex and the City) on her shopping tours through Fifth Avenue buying her 20th pair of Manolo shoes? New York is definitely one of the most cosmopolitan cities of the world and there are many things tourists can discover. Apart from typical sights like the Statue of Liberty, New York food culture is worth talking about. It's influenced by the immigrants who have moved from other countries to New York and have settled there. Eastern European and Italian immigrants have made the city famous for bagles, cheesecake and New York-style pizza. About 4,000 mobile food courts offer food such as falafels and kebabs. But still, hot dogs and pretzels are most popular among the Americans. The city also offers many of the finest haute cuisine restaurants in the United States and you can even find German, Russian or Moroccan restaurants. So you see, New York is absolutely a city worth discovering and visiting!

Task 2: Comprehension

8 points (2 points each)

Answer the questions in full English sentences:

1. When Americans buy food on the streets, what do they like buying most?

____

2. According to the text, are there many expensive restaurants in NY?

____

3. Who has shaped and influenced American food culture?

____

4. Why are the people who have moved from Italy to the USA important?

____

____

Grammar: Passive voice

Task 1: Active or passive?

Decide if the following statements are active (A) or passive (P):

1. Look Tim! The neighbour's dog has just been thrown out of the house. ☐
2. It's incredible! Mum's car has been washed now for almost 45 minutes! ☐
3. Right now Sarah is writing her English homework and eating an apple. ☐
4. In their holidays the tourists were shown the most important sights. ☐
5. After Kelly had finished learning the new words, she watched a DVD. ☐
6. Dad's car is at the garage today. It's being repaired at the moment. ☐

6 points
(1 point each)

Task 2: Passive & tenses

Fill in the verbs in the correct tense, taking care if you need ACTIVE or PASSIVE:

1. Every year New York City ______________________ (*visit*) by many tourists.
2. Many years ago the Statue of Liberty ______________________ (*give*) to NY.
3. Lots of tourists ______________________ (*visit*) the statue since then.
4. After I ______________________ (*see*) the Rockefeller Center, I went to a café.
5. Usually lots of coffee and muffins ______________________ (*sell*) at Starbucks.
6. The USA ______________________ (*never/visit*) by my best friend.
7. In the Statue of Liberty a lift ______________________ (*take*) the tourists up.
8. The World Trade Center ______________________ (*destroy*) by terrorists.
9. Numerous people ______________________ (*die*) in that terror attack.
10. The yellow taxis in New York City ______________________ (*call*) caps.
11. Recently there ______________________ (*be*) lots of traffic jams in NY City.
12. In 5th Avenue money ______________________ (*can/spend*) on shopping.
13. The famous Rockefeller Center ______________________ (*name*) after J. D. Rockefeller.
14. Well-known stars like Madonna ______________________ (*live*) in NY City.
15. In the future the number of people living in NY ______________________ (*rise*).

30 points
(2 points each)

Gesamtpunktezahl

IRREGULAR VERBS, PART 1

base form	past form	past participle	
awake	awoke	awoken	*aufwachen*
be	was/were	been	*sein*
beat	beat	beaten	*schlagen*
become	became	become	*werden*
begin	began	begun	*beginnen*
bet	bet	bet	*wetten*
bite	bit	bitten	*beißen*
bleed	bled	bled	*bluten*
blow	blew	blown	*blasen*
break	broke	broken	*(zer)brechen*
bring	brought	brought	*bringen*
build	built	built	*bauen*
burn	burnt (burned)	burnt (burned)	*verbrennen*
buy	bought	bought	*kaufen*
can/to be able to	could/was able to	–/have been able to	*können*
come	came	come	*kommen*
choose	chose	chosen	*wählen*
cost	cost	cost	*kosten (Geld)*
creep	crept	crept	*kriechen*
cut	cut	cut	*schneiden*
do	did	done	*tun, machen*
deal	dealt	dealt	*handeln/beschäftigen*
dig	dug	dug	*graben*
draw	drew	drawn	*zeichnen*
dream	dreamt (dreamed)	dreamt (dreamed)	*träumen*
drink	drank	drunk	*trinken*
drive	drove	driven	*fahren, lenken*
eat	ate	eaten	*essen, fressen*
fall	fell	fallen	*(nieder)fallen*
feed	fed	fed	*füttern*
feel	felt	felt	*fühlen*
fight	fought	fought	*kämpfen*
find	found	found	*finden*
flee	fled	fled	*flüchten*
fly	flew	flown	*fliegen*
forbid	forbade	forbidden	*verbieten*
forget	forgot	forgotten	*vergessen*
forgive	forgave	forgiven	*vergeben*
freeze	froze	frozen	*(er)/(ein)frieren*
get	got	got	*bekommen, werden*
give	gave	given	*geben*
go	went	gone	*gehen, fahren* (by ...)
grow	grew	grown	*wachsen*
hang	hung	hung	*hängen*
have	had	had	*haben*
hear	heard	heard	*hören*
hide	hid	hidden	*vestecken*
hit	hit	hit	*schlagen*
hold	held	held	*halten*
hurt	hurt	hurt	*verletzen*
keep	kept	kept	*behalten, aufbewahren*
know	knew	known	*kennen, wissen*
lay	laid	laid	*legen*
lead	led	led	*führen*

SCHULARBEITEN

Jetzt wird es ernst! Du hast dich ja schon optimal auf die Schularbeit vorbereitet, alle Vokabeln gelernt, Inhalte durchgelesen und verinnerlicht und jede Menge Grammatikübungen ausgefüllt. Außerdem haben dir die Progress Checks geholfen, einen Überblick über deinen Wissenszuwachs zu bekommen. Nun wartest du nur noch darauf, dein Können endgültig unter Beweis stellen zu dürfen. Aber wie kannst du zu Hause überprüfen, ob du wirklich fit für den nächsten Tag bist? Ganz einfach: Blättere um, und los geht's! Auf den nächsten Seiten findest du **acht** unterschiedliche **Schularbeitsvorschläge** mit jeweils einer Lese- und einer Hörübung sowie Grammatikaufgaben. Klar – bei der Schularbeit musst du ja auch Texte schreiben. Keine Angst: Vorschläge mit passenden Lösungen hierzu findest du am Ende des Buches.

ZEITMANAGEMENT

Gerade bei Schularbeiten ist es besonders wichtig, dass du dir deine Arbeitszeit gut einteilst. Für eine Übungsschularbeit in diesem Buch solltest du nicht länger als **35 bis 40 Minuten** benötigen. Notiere dir, wie lange du brauchst, und überprüfe, ob du das Zeitlimit einhalten kannst!

BEURTEILUNG

Eine Schularbeit in deinem Testbuch wird mit **100 Punkten** beurteilt. Neben jeder Aufgabenstellung findest du ein Punkteschema, mit dem du deine Gesamtpunktezahl errechnen kannst. Vergleiche dein Gesamtergebnis mit dieser Tabelle und voilà: Du weißt, welche Note du erreicht hast.

Punkte	Note
91–100	Sehr gut
80–90	Gut
66–79	Befriedigend
50–65	Genügend
0–49	Nicht genügend

Viel Spaß, gutes Gelingen ... *and don't forget: practice makes perfect!*

Testdauer: 35 min

Schularbeit 1

Listening: A cop and her dog

CD-TRACK 09

Task 1: True or false?

1. Sandra had worked together with other dogs when she met Lakos. ☐
2. She immediately fell for Lakos when she first saw him. ☐
3. Lakos was scared of Sandra at the beginning. ☐
4. Lakos is a very successful police dog. ☐
5. He found drugs worth $ 1.4 million. ☐
6. Lakos once killed a pit bull. ☐
7. When Sandra was attacked by a Rottweiler, Lakos had to give up. ☐
8. Lakos has always been gentle to Sandra's children. ☐
9. He was used as a therapy dog for children whose parents had died. ☐
10. Lakos has become too old to smell drugs now. ☐

15 points (1.5 points each)

Task 2: Key answers

Find the answers to the questions. Do not use more than 4 words.

1. What was Lakos looking for when Sandra first saw him in his cage?

___

2. What did Lakos do to the dog that got him by the tail?

___

3. In how far was Lakos different when he came home from work?

___

4. Why does Sandra believe God sent Lakos to her?

___

5. What is Lakos going to do in his retirement?

___

10 points (2 points each)

Reading: Ireland – magic and mystery

Ireland is definitely a country worth visiting, the only question is how to travel through it. There are different ways, the first possibility is to book a flight to Dublin (the capital) and then make a coach tour by bus. The tour will take you around Ireland, leading you to the most beautiful places and sights like the *Wicklow Mountains*, *Blarney Castle*, *The Ring of Kerry* or *The Cliffs of Moher*. Another option would be to hire a car and discover Ireland on your own. The "Fly and Drive" programme gives you the freedom to go wherever you want and to stop whenever you feel like. If you don't like doing that you might also rent a horse-drawn caravan and travel along quiet country roads. The caravans have space for four people and instructions on how to look after the horse will be given to you. Finally, going through Ireland with a canal boat could also be an option worth thinking about. More than 240 km of quiet water are waiting for you, the only thing you have to do is to hire a boat and enjoy. The boats have got different sizes and are equipped with kitchen and toilets. So just set out and discover this amazing country!

Task 1: Error correction

Correct the following sentences so that they are true according to the text:

1. If you go through Ireland by bus, you'll only be taken to the northern part of the country.

____

2. If you go with a horse-drawn caravan, somebody will look after the horse.

____

3. In case you rent a boat, you only have limited possibilities on where to go.

____

4. On the boats there is only enough space for four people.

____

20 points
(5 points each)

Task 2: True or false?

1. It's a good thing to spend money on a trip to Ireland. ☐

2. You should only go in a horse-drawn caravan if you like horses. ☐

3. If you rent a boat, you cannot go to the toilet on board. ☐

4. The "Fly and Drive" programme gives you a lot of freedom. ☐

5. If you go through Ireland by car, a guide will tell you where to go. ☐

5 points
(1 point each)

Grammar: Past tense and past perfect tense

Task 1: Past tense

Fill in the correct forms of past tense simple or progressive:

The strange case of Hillsbury Castle

My family and I ______________________ (*look*) for a nice house for quite some time. They ______________ (*be*) either too expensive or too small. But then, one day, my dad ________________ (*find*) this big, old house. It ________________ (*call*) "Hillsburry Castle". Wow, what a name! It had three huge floors and a grey roof. A big garden surrounded the house and wild red roses were growing on the sides. We simply loved it and so we immediately ______________ (*move*) in and I soon ______________ (*start*) to explore and discover all the rooms in the house. I ________________________ (*usually/do*) that while mum ________________ (*cook*) dinner. One evening, however, something really scary ______________ (*happen*). I ____________________ (*walk*) through the dark cellar when I suddenly ________________ (*see*) a strange figure. It ____________ (*look*) like a child, only much paler. At first I ______________ (*not know*) what to do but then I __________________ (*take*) a few steps towards the figure. While my feet ________________________ (*slowly/move*), my heart ______________________ (*beat*) very fast. I ______________ (*feel*) afraid and nervous. When I ______________ (*reach*) the strange figure, I suddenly __________________ (*not/can*) see it. Where _________ (*be*) it? ____________ (*be*) I dreaming? In the end it ______________ (*turn*) out that the strange figure was only a light projection and there was absolutely no reason to be afraid. However, while I __________________ (*go*) upstairs my knees ____________________ (*still/shake*) and my hands __________________ (*sweat*). What an adventure at Hillsburry Castle!

25 points
(1 point each)

Task 2: Past or past perfect?

Fill in the correct forms of past tense and past perfect tense:

Have you ever heard about the "Mole people"?

Jennifer Peakston has been a journalist for the "Daily Mirror" for three years and last summer her boss ______________________ (*give*) her a particularly nice story to write about. While being at a party the weekend before he ______________________ (*hear*) about a group of people that live in the tunnels below the streets of New York. He soon ______________________ (*start*) to get interested in the story and after he ______________________ (*get*) back to the office, he ______________________ (*tell*) Jennifer what he ______________________ (*want*) her to do. So Jennifer ___________________ (*leave*) and ________________________ (*make*) herself on the way to the Mole people. She ________________________ (*hear*) about them before and she ____________________________ (*also/read*) a newspaper article once but not more. She ______________________ (*be*) curious and excited but as soon as she ________________________ (*enter*) the tunnel system she ______________________ (*feel*) sick. It was dark and sticky and there was hardly any fresh air. It took Jennifer a few moments to get used to the darkness and to be able to look around. But the bad smell still worried her. Fortunately she ____________________________ (*not/eat*) anything before and so she ___________________________ (*not/must*) throw up. After Jennifer ____________________ (*finally/get*) used to the terrible smell, she ________________ (*start*) her interview with one of the Mole people. His name _______________ (*be*) Mac and he was really dirty and shabby-looking. He ___________________ (*tell*) her lots of strange stories and even ______________________ (*inform*) her about the fact that the Mole people eat rats. At first Jennifer only laughed because she didn't believe him. But then Mac _________________ (*make*) a little demonstration for her. After he ________________________ (*catch*) a big rat with his bare hands, he ________________________ (*throw*) it against the wall. With a loud "crack" it hit the wall and fell onto the ground. Jennifer ____________________ (*can*) hardly look at the scenery. In the end she was only glad when she ____________________ (*can*) leave the tunnels and the Mole people behind.

25 points
(1 point each)

Gesamt-
punktezahl

Testdauer: 35 min

Schularbeit 2

Listening: A witch statue in Salem?

CD-TRACK 10

Task 1: Multiple choice

Tick the correct ending.

1. "Bewitched" is

- **a.** a very popular TV series currently produced in Salem. ☐
- **b.** a TV series that was produced about 40 years ago. ☐
- **c.** a TV series starring Samantha Stephen as a bad witch. ☐

2. Salem is "the center of all things witches" because

- **a.** 19 people were hanged for being accused of practicing witchcraft. ☐
- **b.** the series "Bewitched" was originally produced there. ☐
- **c.** witches there attract many tourists, especially at Halloween. ☐

3. A statue of the "Bewitched" witch Sam should be erected in Salem because

- **a.** it should remind people of the witch trials in the 17th century. ☐
- **b.** it would be good advertisement for the TV series. ☐
- **c.** people think that this statue would be fun. ☐

4. Some people protest against the erection of that statue

- **a.** because they think it is too kitschy. ☐
- **b.** because they do not want occult symbols in their city. ☐
- **c.** because they think that it offends Salem's history. ☐

5. Stanley Usovicz, the mayor of Salem, thinks that

- **a.** the statue would bring many tourists to the town. ☐
- **b.** the city of Salem should pay more tribute to its history. ☐
- **c.** popular culture is nowadays more important than historical culture. ☐

15 points (3 points each)

Task 2: True or false?

1. The TV witch Samantha performed magic by twitching her nose. ☐

2. The statue shows Sam holding her broom under a crescent moon. ☐

3. The people who were hanged 300 years ago confessed being witches. ☐

4. Other statues of TV characters have been erected in the USA. ☐

5. City officials have voted in favour of erecting the statue. ☐

10 points (2 points each)

Reading: Teenage matters

Susie Tompson, 14

I have a problem which has been worrying me for quite some time now. I do swimming lessons three times a week and that's why I don't have a lot of freetime to meet my friends. After school I go straight to the swimming pool where I spend the next three hours working on my swimming technique. I really enjoy swimming at the pool but I would also like to have time to meet friends, go to the movies with them or shopping. I don't have much time because after swim practise I have to go home and do my homework. Kids at my school don't understand why I like to swim so much. My parents say it's good for me and I like it, too. I can't decide whether to keep training so much or to spend more time with my friends. What shall I do, please help me!

Task 1: Spotting the topic

What is the text above about? Tick the correct box.

1. A teenage girl who doesn't know how to become a better swimmer. ☐
2. A teenage girl who has difficulties getting good marks. ☐
3. A teenage girl who is torn between doing sports and meeting friends. ☐

5 points (for the correct answer)

Task 2: Understanding

Read the answer to the girl's problem and put it into the correct order:

☐ What I'd do is talk to my friends about why swimming is so important for me.

☐ This also means deciding whether sports or friends are more important.

☐ They might like swimming, too.

☐ Maybe they can help and support you in your decision.

☐ Susie, I can really understand your problem and I'll try to help you.

☐ Another thing you could do is bring your friends along.

☐ Talk to your parents about how to decide.

☐ If not, you will have to continue to balance your time.

☐ Finally, don't forget to enjoy life and have fun!

☐ Maybe then they will understand.

20 points (2 points each)

Grammar: Infinitive constructions/Conjunctions/ Reported speech

Task 1: Infinitive constructions

Look at the words and form infinitive constructions (I want you to ...). Take care which tense you need!

1. The teachers/their students/to do the home-exercises/regularly

 ____

2. Yesterday/mum/not want/me/help her/in the kitchen

 ____

3. Your best friend/you/to call/her/last weekend?

 ____

4. Usually/Sophie's parents/her/be at home/at nine pm

 ____

5. Clarissa/her boyfriend/take her/to the cinema/Saturday

 ____

5 points
(1 point each)

Task 2: Conjunctions

Fill in a suitable conjunction:

although – because – however – in order to – so that

Which is better – house or apartment?

It's hard to say if living in a house or in a flat is better __________ in both cases there are positive and negative aspects. __________ life in a house might be more attractive, living in an apartment can be very nice, too. There are, __________, also disadvantages. Not having a garden would be an example __________ it's a good thing to have one. __________ a garden is a lot of work, it also makes you feel relaxed. You simply have to take out a comfortable chair __________ have this feeling. Then take a book and a drink __________ you needn't stand up again soon. __________, some flats have balconies __________ people feel like being in a garden. __________ make that work you simply put up some plants.

20 points
(2 points each)

Task 3: Reported speech

My first holiday job – put into reported speech:

Natalie: Philipp, it's nice to meet you! I haven't seen you for ages!
Philipp: Hey Natalie! Are you okay? Do you enjoy your summer holidays?
Natalie: No, not really. I'm working at the moment.
Philipp: Tell me all about it!
Natalie: It's a summer job at my father's office. I usually have to do correspondence work and copy lots of papers.
Philipp: This sounds boring!
Natalie: Yes. But yesterday we had a big party because dad's boss was celebrating his 50th birthday. So we ate cake and drank wine.
Philipp: And will you work there again next summer?
Natalie: I hope I will find something more interesting! Have a nice day Philipp. Bye!

Natalie said to Philipp that ______________________________

______________________________ (3 pts)

Philipp asked Natalie ______________________________

______________________________ (4 pts)

Natalie answered no because ______________________________

______________________________ (2 pts)

Philipp told Natalie ______________________________ (2 pts)

Natalie said that ______________________________

____

______________________________ (4 pts)

Philipp remarked that ______________________________

______________________________ (2 pts)

Natalie said yes and told Philipp that ______________________________

____

______________________________ (4 pts)

Philipp asked Natalie ______________________________

______________________________ (2 pts)

Natalie replied that ______________________________

______________________________ (2 pts)

25 points
(see points in brackets)

Gesamt-
punktezahl

Testdauer:
35 min

Schularbeit 3

Listening: Healthy nutrition

CD-TRACK 11

Task 1: Key answers

Find the answers to the questions. Do not use more than 4 words.

1. Name the three food groups.

a. ______________________________

b. ______________________________

c. ______________________________

2. What do people eat too much of?

a. ______________________________

b. ______________________________

3. What are the consequences of eating too much?

____

4. Who has problems with eating too little?

____

5. Why do they eat too little?

____

6. What happens when you eat too little for a long while?

____

7. What could people eat more to avoid problems?

____

15 points
(1.5 points each)

Task 2: Fill in the missing words.

1. Do these foods give us the full range of ______________ that we need?

2. A healthy diet should be ______________.

3. Couldn't you give our listeners some practical ______________?

4. Being ______________ seriously affects your health.

5. These people have to undergo special medical ______________.

10 points
(2 points each)

Reading: Looking for a job?

Looking for and finding a good job is always difficult. Of course the job should suit and fit you and, probably most important, it should make fun. But where do you find good jobs and how to behave in case you're invited to a job interview? Just go on reading to find out more.
There are several ways how and where to find advertisements for jobs. They might either be posted in newspapers (daily and weekly ones) or on the Internet. Many companies also put job offers on their websites so it's useful to check interesting homepages from time to time. After having found a suitable advertisement for a job, you usually write a so-called letter of application. This is a formal letter to the company you want to work with, in which you present yourself, your education, your personal motivation and your goals. Try to "sell yourself" which means put yourself in the best possible light. You should always use positive adjectives to describe your character, like for instance being reliable, honest, ambitious, patient, hard-working and so on. If the company likes your letter of application, they might invite you to a job interview. Here again, always be polite and try to give your best!

Task 1: Spotting the audience

Who is that text interesting for? Tick the correct box.

1. For people who already have a good job which they like. ☐
2. For people who either don't have a job or look for a new one. ☐
3. For people who are still at school or at university. ☐

5 points (for the correct answer)

Task 2: Comprehension

Answer the questions in full English sentences:

1. According to the text, what characterises a good job? ______________________

____

2. Where can you find job offers? ______________________

____

3. What do I have to do if I want to apply for a job? ______________________

____

4. What should there be in a letter of application? What about the content? ______________________

____

5. What does the term "sell yourself" mean? ______________________

____

20 points (4 points each)

Grammar: Reported questions/Mixed tenses

Task 1: Reported questions

Put the following questions into reported speech:

1. Lisa asked Peter, "Have you ever been unemployed in your life?" ______________________

2. The kids asked their teacher, "Have you got any idea how many problems young teenagers have?" ______________________

3. Melina wanted to know from her mum, "Why are all my friends allowed to stay up longer than I am?" ______________________

4. Colin asked his best friend, "Did you also learn about Australia yesterday?" ______________________

5. Monica asked herself, "What is the teacher talking about?" ______________________

6. Jen wanted to know from her cousin Clara, "Were you afraid when you were in New York all on your own?" ______________________

7. I asked myself, "How can people eat fast food every day?" ______________________

8. Bill asked Sam, "Do you think it's painful to get a tattoo?" ______________________

9. My neighbours asked me, "Did you enjoy your Canal boat holidays in Ireland last summer?" ______________________

10. The English teacher asked me, "What did you like about this book?" ______________________

11. Sue asked Monica, "Do you remember anything from last lesson?" ______________________

22 points
(2 points each)

Task 2: Tenses

Fill in the correct tenses (present/past/present perfect/past perfect/future):

A job interview

Mr Acon: Hello Mrs Mags. Thank you for coming to this job interview. Well, my first question is why ______________________ (*you/want*) to work for "Young Style"?

Mrs Mags: First of all because I __________________ (*think*) it's a fantastic company where I can learn a lot. I also love working with people and it _____________________ (*always/be*) my greatest wish to become a hairdresser.

Mr Acon: I see. ______________________________ (*you/have*) any work experiences?

Mrs Mags: I _____________________ (*have*) several summer jobs so far but I ______________________________ (*not/work*) full time yet.

Mr Acon: Alright. So when __________________________________ (*you/take*) your A-levels?

Mrs Mags: That was last summer. I ________________________________ (*finish*) all my exams at school and then I ___________________ (*take*) some time to travel to England for some weeks in order to improve my English language skills. That was fantastic!

Mr Acon: That __________________ (*sound*) interesting. Mrs Mags, where ____________________ (*you/see*) yourself in five years time?

Mrs Mags: That's a really good question. I'm absolutely sure that in five years time I _________ ____________________________ (*work*) as a professional hairdresser because I'm extremely creative with hair. I think I ____________________ (*have*) lots of fun doing this job in the future and as I ______________________ (*say*) before, it's something I've always wanted to do.

Mr Acon: I can understand that. Thanks for taking your time, Mrs Mags. You will soon hear from our company informing you if you get the job.

28 points
(2 points each)

Gesamtpunktezahl

Testdauer: 35 min

Schularbeit 4

Listening: Australia

CD-TRACK 12

Task 1: Match the texts with the animals.

8 points (2 points each)

1. Text 1 **A** platypus (*Schnabeltier*)

2. Text 2 **B** dingo

3. Text 3 **C** kangaroo

4. Text 4 **D** emu

1	
2	
3	
4	

Task 2: Multiple choice

12 points (3 points each)

1. A platypus is about

- **a.** 55 cm long. ☐
- **b.** 50 km/h fast. ☐
- **c.** 1.7 kilos. ☐

2. Farmers shoot dingoes because

- **a.** they hunt rabbits. ☐
- **b.** they kill their companion animals. (*Nutztiere*) ☐
- **c.** they are dangerous for people. ☐

3. The tallest of the four animals mentioned is

- **a.** the emu. ☐
- **b.** the dingo. ☐
- **c.** the kangaroo. ☐

4. The emu

- **a.** is a very fast runner. ☐
- **b.** has got small but strong wings. ☐
- **c.** has got dark green, two centimetre long eggs. ☐

Task 3: Complete the sentences.

5 points (1 point each)

1. Female kangaroos have a ________________ for carrying their young.

2. The platypus is a ________________ that lays eggs.

3. The kangaroo usually moves by ________________.

4. An emu's egg ________________ more than half a kilo.

5. The platypus has got a ________________ like a duck.

Reading: Amazing fantasy – Spiderman

Today, every child knows and has heard about Spiderman. There are cinema movies, comics, TV series, computer games and so on and it's a comic superhero that is simply part of our everyday life. The character of Spiderman was created by writer-editor Stan Lee and it first appeared in the 1960s. The cinema movie shows a high school student, Peter Parker, who is bitten by a radioactive spider during a science project. As a result Peter, so far the silent and hard-working student, develops spider-like abilities and turns into Spiderman from time to time. As a superhero he has supernatural power and speed as well as the ability to hold on to most surfaces. He can climb walls and he has got spider senses. Amazing, isn't it? Of course, Spiderman has got enemies who he has to fight. We find The Green Goblin, Dr Octopus and Venom among his most dangerous enemies. Like almost all superheroes, Spiderman is strong, brave, full of courage and risks his own life to save others. He is really heroic and he hardly ever feels afraid or insecure.

Task 1: Vocabulary

Match the words with the definitions and fill in the letters next to the numbers.

1. to appear
2. silent
3. an ability
4. enemy
5. heroic

A calm and quiet
B somebody who fights against you
C acting like a hero
D to see something somewhere
E something special you can do

1	
2	
3	
4	
5	

10 points
(2 points each)

Task 2: Characterising somebody

Find and tick the ten adjectives that describe Spiderman's character:

- ☐ bored
- ☐ unreliable
- ☐ courageous
- ☐ weak
- ☐ fearless
- ☐ brave
- ☐ strange
- ☐ sensitive
- ☐ ridiculous
- ☐ unweakened
- ☐ generous
- ☐ lazy
- ☐ moody
- ☐ strong
- ☐ lion-hearted
- ☐ brutal
- ☐ heroic
- ☐ absurd
- ☐ indestructible
- ☐ supernatural

10 points
(1 point each)

Task 3: Complete the sentences.

1. The reason why Peter Parker turns into Spiderman is ______________________________

____.

2. Dr. Octopus is one of Spiderman's biggest ______________________.

5 points
(2.5 points each)

Grammar: Adverbs/Question tags/Present with future meaning

Task 1: Adjective or adverb?

Fill in adjectives (comparisons, too!) or adverbs:

My little brother Kevin

Hello everybody! I'm Sophie and I'm going to tell you about my little brother Kevin. You think this isn't ____________________ (*wirklich*) interesting? Well, wait and see. Kevin is ______________________ (*jünger als*) me and since we were little children we have been quarreling ________________ (*schlimm/schlecht*) with each other. No wonder because life is really __________________ (*hart*) with him. Kevin often turns off my alarm clock so that I oversleep. He then watches me _____________________ (*genau/sorgfältig*) to check if I get _________________ (*böse*). Of course I get because on these days I'm _______________ (*spät*) for school. Sometimes I _______________ (*fast/beinahe*) miss the bus because of his stupidity. It's impossible to tell you how ____________________ (*dumm/blöd*) my brother is and I often have the feeling that even our cat is ____________________________ (*klüger als*) him. Or at least ______________________________ (*genauso klug wie*) he. At school he _______________ (*kaum*) ever talks to me – thank God! From time to time I only see him running around quite _________________ (*schnell*) or talking _________________ (*glücklich*) with some girls. Back at home, however, things get ____________________ (*schwierig*) for me again. He usually finishes his homework _________________ (*schnell*) and then he has lots of time to go on my nerves again. It often takes me ________________ (*länger*) to do my homework so I would need a __________________ (*leise/ruhig*) atmosphere. But in fact Kevin keeps running around ________________ (*wild*) and screaming _________________ (*laut*). It's needless to say that I can't concentrate then. You know, my life is really hard with my little brother Kevin and he's really a pest!

30 points
(1.5 points each)

Task 2: Future meaning

Translate the sentences using present simple tense for the future:

1. Morgen Abend werden meine Familie und ich in ein teures, italienisches Restaurant gehen.

   ___

2. Wann werden wir uns wieder sehen? Am Montag oder am Dienstag?

   ___

3. Am Wochenende wird Joana bei ihren Großeltern auf dem Land sein.

   ___

4. Charles lernt viel, damit er nächstes Jahr besser in Englisch sein wird.

   ___

5. Marc wird seine Freunde um halb acht vor dem Kino treffen.

   ___

10 points
(2 points each)

Task 3: Question tags

Fill in the correct question tags:

1. Aborigines have always lived in Australia, ___?
2. Long ago the Cherokees were driven off their land, ___?
3. We should respect Aborigines, ___?
4. People shouldn't climb the holy mountain "Uluru", ___?
5. The Great Barrier Reef has to be protected, ___?
6. You can go snorkelling and diving at the Reef, ___?
7. Tradition is very important for Native Australians, ___?
8. Sydney isn't the capital of Australia, ___?
9. You didn't ask the tourist guide about crocodiles, ___?
10. We do know a lot about Australia, ___?

10 points
(1 point each)

Gesamtpunktezahl

Testdauer: 35 min

Schularbeit 5

Listening: Collecting more than an obsession for New Yorker

CD-TRACK 13

Task 1: Tick the correct sentences.

1. StoryCorps is a project where Americans talk about their hobbies. ☐
2. Harley Spiller holds a place in the Guinness World Records. ☐
3. There are two rooms in Harley's apartment. ☐
4. Harley likes collecting extraordinary things. ☐
5. He also collects things that sound like his name. ☐
6. Harley got his Harry Spillman baseball card from a child. ☐
7. Harley says that his hobby was inspired by his father. ☐
8. Harley does not collect stamps because there are too many of them. ☐
9. Harley knows that what he is doing is a dangerous obsession. ☐
10. He would not mind if his collection was taken away from him. ☐

10 points (1 point each)

Task 2: Find the numbers.

1. For how many years has Harley been collecting things? ______
2. About how many objects can be found in his apartment? ______
3. How many Chinese menus does he have in his apartment? ______
4. To when does his oldest Chinese menu date back? ______
5. How many chairs does Harley own? ______
6. How many different white plastic spoons does he have? ______
7. The kid who gave Harley his baseball card went to grade …? ______
8. How many minutes did it take him to get the baseball card? ______
9. How many stamps has Harley collected so far? ______
10. How many packs of chewing gum does Harley own? ______

15 points (1.5 points each)

Reading: The day dad's body started to talk

The power of body language – something all of us have already experienced. In my case that happened on the day my dad met my new boyfriend. By the way ... hi, I'm Erica and I'm 30 years old. To make a long story short: I had a wonderful boyfriend who everybody loved, except me. So I left him and got to know somebody else. Somebody who was completely different compared to me. Somebody who my parents could absolutely not handle and that was what my dad expressed the day they met. "Hey there, I'm Hawk", he said, smiling brightly when he was face to face with my father. My dad couldn't have been more unhappy at that moment. He shook hands with Hawk in order to be polite but then he immediately crossed his arms in front of his chest signalising dislike and distance. He didn't smile and his eyes looked serious. His whole body was very stiff and straight and he held his head up high to show how important he was. Hawk, on the other hand, was fully relaxed and the muscles of his body weren't tight at all. It was simply an amazing picture to see the two men standing opposite of each other and communicating via body language.

Task 1: Choose the correct answer.

1. Erica split up with her ex-boyfriend because ...

- **a.** her parents didn't like him. ☐
- **b.** she didn't love him. ☐
- **c.** he didn't come along with Erica's parents and friends. ☐

2. Hawk, Erica's new boyfriend, was ...

- **a.** the complete opposite compared to Erica's ex-boyfriend. ☐
- **b.** the complete opposite to most of Erica's friends. ☐
- **c.** the complete opposite to Erica herself. ☐

3. When comparing the body language of Hawk and Erica's father ...

- **a.** there was a big difference between the two of them. ☐
- **b.** there was hardly any difference to observe. ☐
- **c.** they behaved in the same way and sent out the same signals. ☐

15 points
(5 points each)

Task 2: True or false?

1. Erica's ex-boyfriend was very popular with her family and her friends. ☐

2. Her ex-boyfriend had left Erica because he met another woman. ☐

3. There are really a lot of differences between Erica and Hawk. ☐

4. Erica's dad was not very happy and pleased when he met Hawk. ☐

5. Hawk and Erica's dad liked each other from the beginning onwards. ☐

10 points
(2 points each)

Grammar: Modal verbs/Present perfect or past simple

Task 1: Modal verbs

Find the correct modal verbs. Mind the tenses!

T: Hey Sina. __________ (*dürfen*) I ask you some questions?

S: Sure, Tom! What __________ (*würde*) you like to know?

T: You ______________________ (*haben*) great piercings! When __________________________ (*dürfen – you*) to get your first? ________________________________ (*müssen*) wait long?

S: When I was sixteen, I ______________________ (*nicht können*) wait to have one. But as I _____________________ (*nicht dürfen*) to, I __________ (*müssen*) wait until I was eighteen.

T: I see! I've heard that piercings _______________ (*könnte*) cause problems?

S: That's true! Two days after I had got my forth, it started to hurt terribly and I _________________________ (*nicht können*) twist it any more. That's always a bad sign. I ______________ (*müssen*) take medication and I ____________________________________ (*nicht dürfen*) take baths for quite a while.

T: Are there any rules one __________ (*sollte*) keep in mind?

S: Sure! You _________________________ (*nicht dürfen*) forget to keep them clean and you _________________________ (*nicht sollen*) pierce some special parts of your body.

T: __________ (*würde*) you like to give our readers some more advice?

S: Definitely! If you want to have a piercing, you _______________ (*müssen*) look for a good studio. You _______________ (*könnte*) get infections if the body piercer does not work well. Of course, you _______________ (*können*) always ask one of your friends if they know a good one. You ___________________________________ (*nicht müssen*) ask your parents for permission when you are 18, but I __________ (*würde*) always inform them. You ___________ (*könnte*) also take a friend to the studio because you __________ (*könnte*) possibly feel nervous. However, you _________________________________ (*nicht müssen*) be afraid if you have a good studio. You _________________________ (*nicht dürfen*) forget: It's your choice!

25 points
(1 point each)

Task 2: Present perfect or past simple?

Translate the following sentences.

1. Oh nein! Dieser Mann hat uns soeben ausgeraubt!

____

2. Haben Sie den Zwischenfall schon der Polizei gemeldet?

____

3. Wann hast du zuletzt so eine tragische Geschichte gehört?

____

4. We lange spielt ihr schon Verstecken?

____

5. Hast du gestern den Installateur gerufen?

____

10 points
(2 points each)

Task 3: Present perfect or past simple?

Fill in the verbs in the correct tense.

Sam: Sorry, I'm late. ____________________ (*you – have*) wait long?

Pat: No, I ____________________ (*just – arrive*) too.

Sam: ______________________________ (*you – already – order*)? I am so hungry, I ________________ (*not eat*) since 10! I ________________ (*be*) in a hurry all day.

Pat: Oh dear! The waiter ____________________________ (*not yet – take my order*).

Sam: Okay. Let's start with the interview. Tell me, Pat, when ____________________ (*you – start*) extreme ironing?

Pat: I first __________ (*hear*) about it ten years ago, but I only __________ (*try*) it for the first time in 2004. I immediately __________ (*fall*) for it.

Sam: So, at which crazy places ____________________________ (*you – already – iron*)?

Pat: Oh, last year, I __________ (*do*) it in the Pacific Ocean, and two years ago we __________ (*must*) climb rocks on the French Côte d'Azur.

Sam: Cool! ______________________________ (*you – ever – win*) a prize?

Pat: Yeah! Two years ago, I __________ (*make*) the first place!

15 points
(1 point each)

Gesamt-
punktezahl

Schularbeit 6

Testdauer:
35 min

Listening: Reading habits

CD-TRACK 14

Task 1: Find the mistake and write down the correct sentence.

1. Robin likes reading very much.

____

2. Robin read most of Jane Eyre.

____

3. Paul likes reading on the bus.

____

4. Paul likes reading about other people's interests.

____

5. Gisela rarely has a book with her.

____

6. Gisela prefers watching a film to reading a book.

____

15 points
(2.5 points each)

Task 2: Multiple choice

1. Robin
   - a. did not hand in most of his homework on Jane Eyre. ☐
   - b. copied his homework on Jane Eyre from his brother. ☐
   - c. did not read most of the book Jane Eyre. ☐
2. Paul
   - a. can't read on the bus because he gets sick. ☐
   - b. really needs to concentrate when he reads. ☐
   - c. does not have a lot of time to read on holiday. ☐
3. Gisela
   - a. does not like reading at school because people interrupt her. ☐
   - b. prefers films to books because pictures are more vivid there. ☐
   - c. sees pictures in her head as if they were a movie when she reads. ☐

10 points
(3.3 points each)

Reading: Fair trade for a fair world

Tim Rug: Mrs Meyers, which types of fair trade products are there?
Mrs Meyers: There are different products like sweets, tea, coffee, fruit, rice and even oil.
Tim Rug: How exactly do people know if they buy fair trade products?
Mrs Meyers: That's easy to find out. Every of these products has a blue/green/black sticker on it that says it's fair trade. I'm sure you have already seen this.
Tim Rug: Why should people buy fair trade products?
Mrs Meyers: Because they guarantee you that the products were produced under fair conditions and the workers get enough money for their work.
Tim Rug: Are there any quality criteria for fair trade products?
Mrs Meyers: Well, there is a controlling system that checks all the products on a regular basis. This makes sure that the customers only get first-class quality products.
Tim Rug: Thanks a lot Mrs Meyers. That was a really interesting conversation.

Task 1: Gap-filling

Complete this summary with the words given (there are 3 extra words!):

cover – good – easy – produced – famous – sticker – paid – bad – difficult

Fair trade products are ______________________ under fair conditions. This means that the workers are treated and ______________ fair and so they have enough money to live. It's ______________ to find out if a product is fair trade or not because it is marked with a ______________. People don't have to worry that the quality of fair trade products is ______________ as there are regular checks. Fair trade chocolate is probably most ______________ but there are other products (like rice and oil), too.

18 points
(3 points each)

Task 2: Matching sentence halves

It's always a good thing to	easy to find and recognise.
When buying such products,	products is really wide.
This is important because they	workers are supported.
Fair trade products are	is green, blue and black.
The sticker that marks them	buy fair trade products.
The product range of fair trade	chocolate to rice, fruit and even oil.
You can have everything from	don't earn much money anyway.

7 points
(1 point each)

Grammar: Conditionals/Pronouns

Task 1: Conditionals

Fill in the correct forms of the verbs.

1. I would help you if I ______________ (*have*) time.
2. Every newborn baby ______________ (*swim*) if you put it into water.
3. Zac __________________________ (*not feel*) so bad if he had not forgotten to meet you.
4. You can help many people if you ____________ (*buy*) fair trade products.
5. What __________________________ (*you – do*) if you were in my situation?
6. If Joe fails the test again, he __________________________ (*not pass*) this year!
7. Honeypuff would not cry for food now if you ______________ (*feed*) her.
8. If you throw a boomerang properly, it ______________ (*come*) back to you.
9. I ____________________ (*never – tell*) anyone if you do not want me to.
10. If I knew how, I ______________ (*ask*) Tonya out.

10 points
(1 point each)

Task 2: Mixed conditionals

Read the example sentences. Then write matching conditional sentences.

1. John didn't study for the test. So, he failed. (If – study more: not fail) ____________________

   ____

2. It is raining. I probably won't go for a walk. (If – not rain: go for a walk) ________________

   ____

3. If – leave ice-cream – sun: melt ____

   ____

4. Tim forgot to invite Gina. He feels bad now. (If – not forget: not feel bad) ______________

   ____

5. Alicia doesn't want to invite Mary to her party. (If – not invite: Mary sad) ______________

   ____

15 points
(3 points each)

Task 3: Reflexive pronouns

Fill in the correct reflexive pronoun.

Kelly: Have you ever asked ______________________ if you read enough?

Doug: Sure. But I have to say that I wouldn't call __________ a bookworm.

Kelly: But most people enjoy ______________________ when they read a good book.

Doug: I know. However, my friend Miley and I consider ______________________ more the TV-watching kind than the reading kind of persons.

Kelly: What was the last book you bought ______________________?

Doug: That was "Harry Potter and the deathly hollows". I have to say, the story __________ was quite good, but I think the book was a bit too long.

Kelly: Thank you for the interview!

15 points
(2.5 points each)

Task 4: Pronouns

Fill in any pronoun or article that fits.

Good morning everybody!

Today, I want to talk about __________ favourite book. __________ name is "Twilight".

I have to say, I was not into vampires before. But one day, my sister Daphne and I found ______________________ in front of this book shop – and there it was: The first volume of the "Twilight Saga". We wanted to give it a try and: I really saw __________ spellbound from the first page on. We bought two copies for ______________________, and one for our mum. I finished __________ in a week and Daphne __________ in two. Our mum, however, really surprised us all: She finished __________ copy within two days! She really found __________ drawn into the story from the first page on – and she simply could not let go of the book until she had finished the last page. Isn't that funny?

So, this is my experience with "Twilight". What is __________?

10 points
(1 point each)

Gesamt-
punktezahl

Testdauer: 35 min

Schularbeit 7

Listening: Festival fun

CD-TRACK 15

Task 1: Key answers

Find the answers to the questions. Do not use more than 4 words.

1. Why is a trip to Disney Land a nightmare for some people?

____

2. Where does the Neighbourhood Boys and Girls Club's Fest take place?

____

3. What happens with most of the money earned at that festival?

____

4. In how far is that festival different to Disney World, according to Ms Carle?

____

5. How does Michael Schaper feel after a ride on Zero Gravity?

____

10 points (2 points each)

Task 2: True or false?

1. The Neighbourhood Boys and Girls Club's Fest takes place in a park. ☐
2. You can win live goldfish and Disney character stuffed animals there. ☐
3. The ride and game operators are very polite there. ☐
4. Ms Carle's children are riding on a slow mini Ferris-wheel. ☐
5. She wants to go to Disney World some day. ☐
6. 4-year-old Rebecca Byrnes loves her stay at the festival. ☐
7. Michael, the presenter's son, has never been to Disney World. ☐
8. You get unlimited rides for four hours for 15 dollars. ☐
9. Michael enjoys his stay at the festival a lot. ☐
10. The food at the festival is very healthy. ☐

15 points (1.5 points each)

Reading: Believe it or not – UFO sighting

I'm Brian and I live in California. I'm 43 years old and I work as a plumber. My friends and family would most probably describe me as normal and conventional and that's what I am. I've never done anything strange or crazy and I'm just a regular guy. So don't call me a madman or an idiot when I now tell you what happened to me some weeks ago. It was Thursday evening, already past 7 pm. I was on the highway finally driving home after a long day of work. The sky was clear and bright, it was full moon and you could see the stars. I quite like looking at the night sky because that relaxes me a lot. What I saw, however, fascinated and shocked me at the same time. I saw ten red lights travelling, one by one, through the sky. I stopped my car to take a closer look and spent the next 20–30 minutes watching and observing these lights. They didn't make any sound and were flying as high as a helicopter might fly. I felt excited and afraid but I managed to take some pictures with my mobile. I zoomed in and saw that there was no other shape than the lights. What was that? And was I the only one who saw these strange lights? Well, so many unanswered questions ...

Task 1: Error correction

Correct the following sentences so that they are true according to the text:

1. It makes Brian feel tired to watch the sky and he doesn't like doing that.

____

2. When Brian saw the red lights he was on his way to work.

____

3. The red lights were flying much higher than a helicopter would.

____

4. Brian could take some pictures of the flying lights with his camera.

____

5. Brian only watched the flying lights for a few minutes.

____

20 points
(4 points each)

Task 2: Spotting the topic

What is the text above about? Tick the correct box.

1. A man who has seen a UFO and now doesn't tell it to anybody. ☐

2. A man who has seen a UFO and now doesn't know what to do. ☐

3. A man who has seen a UFO and now doesn't look at the sky anymore. ☐

5 points
(for the correct answer)

Grammar: Phrasal verbs/Adjective or adverb

Task 1: Phrasal verbs

Match the phrasal verbs with their meanings.

1. to sort out
2. to go on
3. to get on with sb.
4. to pick up sth.
5. to go out with sb.
6. to hang around
7. to find out
8. to bump into
9. to look at
10. to look for

A to develop, to continue
B to discover more about a subject
C to become someone's boy/girlfriend
D to happen to meet someone
E to watch
F to have a good relationship with sb.
G to search for
H to stay in a place, doing nothing
I to find a solution to a problem
J to buy something on the go

1	
2	
3	
4	
5	
6	
7	
8	
9	
10	

10 points
(1 point each)

Task 2: Phrasal verbs

Complete the dialogue with the correct phrasal verb.

Chris: So, how are you ____________ ______ with Sienna?

Rick: Oh, not well. I think we might ____________ ______ soon.

Chris: So, you haven't been able to ____________ ______ your problems?

Rick: No, see: I saw her ____________ ______ in the shopping mall with some other guy.

Chris: That's too bad! But are you sure that she is ____________ ______ with that guy? What if she just was ____________ ______ something in the mall and then ____________ ______ that boy.

Rick: I don't think so. She was ____________ ______ him with that strange, dreamy look.

Chris: Oh, I'm sorry for you! However, you should really talk to Sienna and try to ____________ ______ if she is serious with that other guy.

Rick: I know. I can't ______ ______ making guesses. I should talk to her and find out what's going on.

15 points
(1.5 points each)

Task 3: Adjective or adverb?

Find the correct word for the German term in brackets.

Hi Jennifer,

Sorry for answering your e-mail so ________________ (*spät*). I've been very busy ________________ (*in letzter Zeit*). How are things going on in Atlanta? Are you still working ________________ (*hart*) on your essay on Native Americans?

Things are going on ________________ (*gut*) for me. Imagine! Last week, I was at Frequency Festival in St. Pölten. That was a ________________ (*fantastisch*) experience. I went there with some of my friends. When we arrived at the carpark, there was a ________________ (*groß*) crowd waiting. So we really had to rush ________________ (*schnell*) to the festival area. There was already playing ________________ (*laut*) music and as it was ________________ (*extrem*) hot, the air already smelled ________________ (*schlecht*). First, we ________________ (*sorfältig*) checked out the area and then we studied the line-up. The first band we wanted to see was Franz Ferdinand. Their show was ________________ (*absolut*) great and they gave a really ________________ (*gut*) performance of some of their older songs. After the show, I got ________________ (*furchtbar*) hungry. I ________________ (*schnell*) found a stand that sold chilli con carne. It looked a bit ________________ (*seltsam*), but it tasted ________________ (*wonderful*). I offered some to Michael, who only tasted it ________________ (*zögerlich*: reluctant), but he liked it too. However, he started feeling ________________ (*schlecht*) and dashed off to the toilet. There, he ________________ (*hektisch*) jumped the queue. The other people waiting there looked at him ________________ (*wütend*). I was ________________ (*ziemlich*) sure that Michael's problems had nothing to do with the chilli, but he insisted ________________ (*stur*: stubborn) that the chilli had gone ________________ (*schlecht*). We could ________________ (*kaum*) convince him to get back to the concerts. However, after two hours …

25 points
(1 point each)

Gesamt-
punktezahl

Testdauer:
40 min

Schularbeit 8

Listening: The history of New York's taxicabs

CD-TRACK 16

Task 1: Multiple choice

1. New Yorkers
   - **a.** are happy to celebrate their taxicabs' 100th birthday. ☐
   - **b.** hate riding a taxi. ☐
   - **c.** find it difficult to get a taxi when they need one. ☐

2. Graham Hodge, who wrote a book on the history of New York's taxicabs,
   - **a.** is a taxi driver. ☐
   - **b.** gives lectures on history. ☐
   - **c.** is 70 years old. ☐

3. Harry N. Allen
   - **a.** imported 56 cabs from Europe. ☐
   - **b.** founded a taxicab business because he was angry about high prices. ☐
   - **c.** introduced the first taxicabs in 1907. ☐

4. Cab drivers in films of the 50s were presented
   - **a.** as helpful and communicative. ☐
   - **b.** as criminals and drug addicts. ☐
   - **c.** as aggressive and fast drivers. ☐

5. Which sentence describes nowadays taxi drivers best?
   - **a.** They love talking about their families. ☐
   - **b.** They mainly have an immigrant background. ☐
   - **c.** They are seen as an integral part of the New York City society. ☐

15 points
(3 points each)

Task 2: Complete the sentences.

1. You can always find a cab until you ______________ one.
2. People have sort of a love-hate ______________________ to taxi drivers.
3. As a taxi driver you could make some ____________ money in the 1920s.
4. In the 1950s, the colour of the cabs finally changed to ______________.
5. Nowadays, most taxi drivers are not qualified or ______________.

10 points
(2 points each)

Reading: Saving our planet with the 5 Rs

Greg: Tina, at your school you've organised a great project in order to help save the environment. Can you tell me something about it because it really sounds interesting!

Tina: Sure! It's a campaign that informs people about the 5 Rs.

Greg: The 5 Rs? What are they? Please tell me!

Tina: Well, they are *reduce*, *reuse*, *recycle*, *refuse* and *repair*. Reduce means that people should try to reduce the number of waste. Reuse is using things again, like filling up bottles for example. Recycling is clear anyway. You are most likely to recycle cans, glass and paper. Refuse means that you can bring along your own shopping bag for example and refuse a plastic bag. That's very easy. And repair, finally, means repairing your things and not immediately throwing them away like most people do these days.

Greg: Sounds interesting. And what exactly did you do in your campaign?

Tina: We drew posters and banners and went through the streets informing people and talking with them about what they can change and how they can help.

Greg: Super! Sounds like a really good thing you did! All the best for your future!

Tina: Thanks a lot!

Task 1: Locate the text.

Where would you most probably find a text like that?

1. In the local section of a daily newspaper. ☐
2. In a book about how to save planet Earth. ☐
3. In a school magazine or an annual school report. ☐

5 points (for the correct answer)

Task 2: True or false?

1. Tina attends university. ☐
2. She doesn't seem to be interested in nature and the environment. ☐
3. She went on strike to show people how to save the environment. ☐
4. The 5 Rs are a good way to help and protect our environment. ☐
5. *Refuse* means you refuse to make any waste. ☐
6. *Repair* means you exchange old things through new ones. ☐
7. It's really simple to bring along your own shopping bag. ☐
8. It's easy to collect and then recycle glass and cans. ☐
9. Tina's project was basically an information campaign. ☐
10. Tina's group told the people in the streets how to do their shopping. ☐

20 points (2 points each)

Grammar: Passive voice

Task 1: Passive voice

Write a text about White Cloud, a Native American girl. Use passive voice.

geboren: 1862
von Mutter und Vater sehr geliebt
Mutter: gezeigt, wie man Fleisch trocknet
von Vater mitgenommen: Tiere beobachten
4 Jahre: Eltern von Weißen getötet
Medizinmann: Rituale und Geschichten gelehrt
von vielen um Hilfe bei Problemen gefragt

9 Jahre: von Weißen weggebracht
neuer Name
Haare abgeschnitten
seltsame Kleidung angezogen
in katholische Schule geschickt
als weißes Mädchen aufgezogen
17: mit weißem Mann verheiratet

This is the story of White Cloud, a Native American girl ____________________

25 points (minus 1 per mistake)

Task 2: Active or passive?

Read the dialogue. Then put the verbs in brackets in active or passive voice. Mind the tenses!

Page: Hi Summer! I ______________ (*tell*) that you ______________ (*win*) a trip to New York at our last prom! That's incredible!

Summer: Yeah, imagine: I ______________ (*wait*) at the tombola, not really expecting ______________ (*call*), when suddenly my name ______________ (*read*) out loudly and clearly. I ______________ (*feel*) so overwhelmed I nearly ______________ (*cry*).

Page: With whom ______________ (*go – you*) there?

Summer: I ______________ (*ask*) by Dave first, but then I ______________ (*decide*) to go with Rick. You know … I ______________ (*have*) a crush on him.

Page: How ______________ (*be*) the journey?

Summer: Imagine! When we ______________ (*step*) out of the airport, a stretch coach ____________________ (*wait*) for us! While we ____________________ (*take*) to the hotel, we ____________________ (*offer*) drinks and appetisers.

Page: ______________ (*you – see*) any stars in New York?

Summer: You can bet on that! On the third day, after Rick and I ________________________ (*just – take*) on a sightseeing tour through Manhattan, we ______________ (*enter*) our hotel and BANG – Robert Pattinson and Kristen Stewart! They ____________________________ (*interview*), so Rick and I ____________________ (*not want*) to disturb them.

Page: I see. But ______________ (*tell*) me: ____________________________________ (*anything – happen*) between you and Rick? Every time you ______________ (*mention*) him your eyes start to sparkle.

Summer: Hmm – since we came home I ____________________________________ (*ask out*) three times …

25 points
(1 point each)

Gesamt-
punktezahl

BILDUNGSSTANDARDS

Was sind Bildungsstandards?

Bildungsstandards für Fremdsprachen legen fest, welche Kompetenzen und Fertigkeiten ein Schüler am Ende der 8. Schulstufe (also der 4. Klasse AHS/HS/NMS) im Fach Englisch nachhaltig (langfristig) erworben haben soll. Sie definieren daher sprachliche Kompetenz und liefern Rückmeldung darüber, wie erbrachte Leistungen zu bewerten sind. Bildungsstandards erfordern – wie uns der Name schon verrät – **standardisierte Testformate** und bieten dadurch gute Vergleichsmöglichkeiten zwischen Klassen-, Schul- und nationalen Ergebnissen. Konkret heißt das also, dass – egal von welcher Form der Unterstufe Schülerinnen und Schüler kommen – sie am Ende der vierten Klasse gleiche Levels/Niveaus haben sollten. Und genau dabei hilft dir dieses Testbuch! Die Testformate entsprechen den 2009 vom Bundesministerium verordneten Bildungsstandards und bereiten dich bestmöglich auf standardisierte Testungen vor.

Testformate bei den Bildungsstandards

Doch welches sind nun diese eben beschriebenen standardisierten Testformate? Hier ein kleiner Überblick:

Hören

- Du solltest Anweisungen/Fragen/Auskünfte/Erzählungen und Mitteilungen in einem sprachlich vertrauten Kontext verstehen können.
- Wenn deutlich gesprochen wird, kannst du die wichtigsten Punkte in Audio- und Videoaufnahmen erfassen.

Das Format der Aufgabenstellungen entspricht *Multiple-Choice*-Übungen mit vier zur Auswahl stehenden Antworten.

Lesen

- Einfache, klar gegliederte Texte zu vertrauten Themen in Zeitungen und Zeitschriften werden im Wesentlichen verstanden. Relevante und wichtige Informationen können herausgefiltert werden.
- Du bist in der Lage, Informationen in Prospekten/Speisekarten/Fahrplänen usw. richtig zu lesen und zu deuten.

Typische Aufgabenstellungen den Bildungsstandards entsprechend sind zB:
Tick the correct answer / What is the text about? / Who is it written for?/ Where do you find a text like that? / Matching sentences / Matching headlines

An Gesprächen teilnehmen

- Zu einem bestimmten Thema bist du in der Lage, Zustimmungen zu äußern beziehungsweise zu widersprechen und andere Vorschläge zu machen.
- Du kannst Anweisungen geben (zB den Weg erklären) und einfache Vereinbarungen treffen.
- Vertraute Alltagssituationen zu bewältigen, sollte für dich kein Problem sein (beispielsweise in einem Restaurant oder Geschäft).

Zusammenhängend sprechen

- Du solltest in der Lage sein, über deinen Alltag und vertraute Sachverhalte/Abläufe Auskunft zu geben (zB Leute beschreiben, über den letzten Urlaub reden, tägliche Routinen beschreiben usw.).
- Eine Geschichte zu erzählen (entweder eine reale oder eine erfundene), sollte kein wirkliches Problem für dich darstellen.

Für den mündlichen Teil der Bildungsstandards solltest du in jedem Fall mit dem Vokabular für folgende Themenbereiche vertraut sein:

Familie/Freunde, Wohnen/Umgebung, Essen/Trinken, Kleidung, Körper/Gesundheit, Jahres-/Tagesablauf, Feste/Ferien, Schule/Arbeitswelt, Hobbys/Interessen, Erlebnisse, Umwelt/Gesellschaft, Medien/Literatur.

Schreiben

- Einfache fiktionale (also erfundene) Geschichten sollten geschrieben werden können.
- Du solltest in schriftlicher Form über deine Familie, dein Umfeld (Heim, Schule, Hobbys usw.) und andere Menschen Auskunft geben können.
- Ebenso solltest du Gefühle und Reaktionen beschreiben und ausdrücken können.

Wichtig bei diesem Teil der Bildungsstandards ist, dass die **Textsorte richtig erkannt** wird (also zum Beispiel Postkarte, Brief, Interview, Geschichte), dass die **Aufgabenstellung mit den inhaltlichen Vorgaben erfüllt** wird (worüber sollst du eigentlich schreiben?) und dass die **vorgegebene Textlänge nicht überschritten** wird.

Beurteilung

In diesem Testbuch findest du zu den Bildungsstandards passende Hör- und Leseübungen, die jeweils wieder mit einem Punktesystem beurteilt werden.

HÖRÜBUNGEN

ZEITMANAGEMENT

Wie bei der Überprüfung der Bildungsstandards gilt es auch hier, **alle Hörübungen zügig hintereinander** zu **erledigen**. Schau genau auf die Stoppuhr, denn nur dann erhältst du ein aussagekräftiges Ergebnis. Anweisungen zu Zeitangaben findest du bei jeder Übung.

BEURTEILUNG

Für jede richtige Antwort erhältst du einen Punkt. Addiere alle erreichten Punkte und vergleiche sie mit dieser Tabelle.

Punkte	Note
36–40	Sehr gut
32–35	Gut
27–31	Befriedigend
21–26	Genügend
0–20	Nicht genügend

LESEÜBUNGEN

ZEITMANAGEMENT

Auch bei den Leseübungen ist dir ein strenger **Zeitrahmen** auferlegt. Zeitangaben findest du bei jeder Übung. Am Ende dieser Zeit stoppst du, vergleichst deine Lösungen und rechnest alle erreichten Punkte zusammen. Die Tabelle zeigt dir dein Ergebnis.

Punkte	Note
50–55	Sehr gut
44–49	Gut
36–43	Befriedigend
28–35	Genügend
0–27	Nicht genügend

Standardisierte Aufgaben zum Bereich HÖREN

LC 1: Your personal well-being

CD-TRACK 17

1. Read the task. You have got 45 seconds.
2. Listen to the presentation and tick the correct answers.
3. Check your answers for 45 seconds.
4. Listen to the presentation for a second time.
5. Check your answers for 45 seconds. Then do the next task.

1. Looking at the scales all the time
   - ☐ helps you to keep track of your weight.
   - ☐ does not make you feel good and self-assured.
   - ☐ helps you to lose pounds and kilos.
   - ☐ helps you to feel less self-conscious.

2. Watching television makes you eat more
   - ☐ candy-bars and crisps.
   - ☐ chips and sweets.
   - ☐ potatoes and crisps.
   - ☐ snacks with a lot of calories.

3. You should try to meet people who
   - ☐ are attractive.
   - ☐ do not care at all about their appearance.
   - ☐ have a positive picture of themselves.
   - ☐ worry about many problems.

4. When you stand up straight
   - ☐ you look happier.
   - ☐ you look heavier.
   - ☐ your stomach muscles get stronger.
   - ☐ people think you have a strong character.

5. It is good for you
   - ☐ to look at photos of you that you do not like.
   - ☐ to have relaxing evenings on your couch.
   - ☐ to think of moments when you really felt great.
   - ☐ to tell your friends what you do not like about them.

5 points
(1 point each)

LC 2: Visiting Australia

CD-TRACK 18

1. Read the task. You have got 45 seconds.
2. Listen to the interview and tick the correct answers.
3. Check your answers for 45 seconds.
4. Listen to the interview for a second time.
5. Check your answers for 45 seconds. Then do the next task.

1. Gisela thought that her trip to Australia was the
   - ☐ most exceptional trip she has ever had.
   - ☐ most unconventional trip she has ever had.
   - ☐ most emotional trip she has ever had.
   - ☐ most sensational trip she has ever had.

2. Perth is in the
   - ☐ east of Australia.
   - ☐ west of Australia.
   - ☐ north of Australia.
   - ☐ south of Australia.

3. At one beach where the water was not very deep
   - ☐ Gisela swam with dolphins.
   - ☐ Gisela got a fish from a dolphin.
   - ☐ Gisela was not allowed to feed the dolphins.
   - ☐ Gisela touched dolphins.

4. Gisela thought that swimming with dolphins
   - ☐ was amazing.
   - ☐ was entertaining.
   - ☐ was dangerous.
   - ☐ was fantastic.

5. At the Eighty Mile Beach
   - ☐ you find a great place for snorkelling.
   - ☐ you find wonderful rock formations.
   - ☐ you can enjoy an amazing scenery.
   - ☐ you can find an extremely long, white sandy beach.

5 points
(1 point each)

LC 3: My favourite food

CD-TRACK 19

1. Read the task. You have got 45 seconds.
2. Listen to the interview and tick the correct answers.
3. Check your answers for 45 seconds.
4. Listen to the interview for a second time.
5. Check your answers for 45 seconds. Then do the next task.

1. What does Lizzy think about vanilla ice-cream with hot raspberries?
   - ☐ She prefers chocolate-cream.
   - ☐ It is one of her favourites.
   - ☐ She does not like it at all.
   - ☐ She thinks it's fun to eat it.

2. Lizzy says about cheese
   - ☐ that she likes the smell of it.
   - ☐ that it spoils her pizza.
   - ☐ that she only accepts it on pizza.
   - ☐ that she would never eat anything with cheese on it.

3. Anna says that she is a vegetarian
   - ☐ because she does not miss eating meat.
   - ☐ because she does not like the taste of any kind of meat.
   - ☐ because she prefers fruit, vegetables cakes and desserts.
   - ☐ because she does not want animals to suffer for her.

4. Paul
   - ☐ eats a lot and puts on weight easily.
   - ☐ always feels hungry and therefore eats a lot of meat.
   - ☐ eats a lot of junk food and unhealthy food.
   - ☐ thinks that drinking half a litre of soft drinks is enough.

5. Who has got a sweet tooth?
   - ☐ Lizzy and Anna
   - ☐ Only Paul
   - ☐ Lizzy and Paul
   - ☐ all three of them

5 points
(1 point each)

LC 4: Total eclipse

CD-TRACK 20

1. Read the task. You have got 45 seconds.
2. Listen to the interview and tick the correct answers.
3. Check your answers for 45 seconds.
4. Listen to the interview for a second time.
5. Check your answers for 45 seconds. Then do the next task.

1. When did the total eclipse of the sun take place?
   - ☐ On August, 11th, 1998
   - ☐ On August, 1st, 1999
   - ☐ On August, 11th, 1999
   - ☐ On August, 1st, 1998

2. In Salzburg
   - ☐ Nicki had a perfect view of the eclipse.
   - ☐ the light was too bright for being able to see the eclipse.
   - ☐ there were no clouds in the sky.
   - ☐ you couldn't see the corona.

3. 30% of the sun were still visible
   - ☐ in Spain.
   - ☐ in Styria.
   - ☐ in Slovakia.
   - ☐ in Sophia.

4. The weather was too bad to see anything of the eclipse in
   - ☐ Spain.
   - ☐ Graz.
   - ☐ Britain.
   - ☐ Munich.

5. There were only partial eclipses
   - ☐ only in Spain.
   - ☐ in Graz and Salzburg.
   - ☐ in Spain and Vienna.
   - ☐ in Britain and Vienna.

5 points
(1 point each)

LC 5: Being a Leo

CD-TRACK 21

1. Read the task. You have got 45 seconds.
2. Listen to the presentation and tick the correct answers.
3. Check your answers for 45 seconds.
4. Listen to the presentation for a second time.
5. Check your answers for 45 seconds. Then do the next task.

1. Leos

- [ ] love fun, but they want things to go their way.
- [ ] enjoy life and do not mind being lied to.
- [ ] love to work a lot.
- [ ] are honest, but they do not like giving things away.

2. One of their negative sides is that they can sometimes be too

- [ ] busy.
- [ ] beasty.
- [ ] boozy.
- [ ] bossy.

3. From February to May

- [ ] finances may get out of order.
- [ ] Leos will have hardly any work to do.
- [ ] Leos should try to get to know new people.
- [ ] their love life will somehow sort out.

4. Leos should not rush solving problems in

- [ ] April.
- [ ] January.
- [ ] July.
- [ ] June.

5. On June 16th

- [ ] the full moon will trouble finances.
- [ ] a Leo's love life will be troubled.
- [ ] nothing will work out fine.
- [ ] Leos will get a visit from a friendly relative.

5 points
(1 point each)

LC 6: Australian Aborigines

CD-TRACK 22

1. Read the task. You have got 45 seconds.
2. Listen to the presentation and tick the correct answers.
3. Check your answers for 45 seconds.
4. Listen to the presentation for a second time.
5. Check your answers for 45 seconds. Then do the next task.

1. How many Aborigines live in Australia?
   - ☐ 250 000
   - ☐ 250
   - ☐ 2 500 000
   - ☐ 2 500

2. Where does the majority of Aborigines live?
   - ☐ as nomads in the Northern territory
   - ☐ in reservation following their old traditions
   - ☐ in cities
   - ☐ on sheep farms

3. Aborigines speak
   - ☐ English.
   - ☐ the same language.
   - ☐ several thousand dialects.
   - ☐ many different dialects.

4. Aborigines
   - ☐ have got great agricultural skills.
   - ☐ use bows and arrows to hunt and to fish.
   - ☐ often walk through the country and build simple shelters.
   - ☐ build strong as well as colourful houses.

5. When a boy becomes a man
   - ☐ he makes stone tools.
   - ☐ he has to undergo ceremonies.
   - ☐ he has to create a rock painting.
   - ☐ he has to prove that he is just one part of nature.

5 points
(1 point each)

LC 7: My favourite book

CD-TRACK 23

1. Read the task. You have got 45 seconds.
2. Listen to the interview and tick the correct answers.
3. Check your answers for 45 seconds.
4. Listen to the interview for a second time.
5. Check your answers for 45 seconds. Then do the next task.

1. The interview is about a book called
   - ☐ My Right Foot.
   - ☐ My Left Food.
   - ☐ My Last Loot.
   - ☐ My Left Foot.

2. In this book
   - ☐ someone writes about the author's life.
   - ☐ the author writes the true story of someone with a spastic illness.
   - ☐ the author writes about his own experiences with an illness.
   - ☐ Christy Brown makes up a story of a man with an illness.

3. What is special about the person presented in the story?
   - ☐ He learned to use his left foot to write and draw.
   - ☐ He learned to use his left foot to dance.
   - ☐ He learned to gradually move his left foot.
   - ☐ He learned to use his left foot to eat.

4. How did the reader feel about the story?
   - ☐ just depressed and frustrated
   - ☐ always sympathetic and sorry for the writer
   - ☐ the reader's mood reflected the mood of the writer
   - ☐ the reader did not feel much

5. Why does the reader recommend the book?
   - ☐ because it teaches you a lot of new insight
   - ☐ because you learn to feel sympathy for handicapped people
   - ☐ because it opens your mind and soul
   - ☐ because you realise how much you know about handicapped people

5 points
(1 point each)

LC 8: The future of our planet

CD-TRACK 24

1. Read the task. You have got 45 seconds.
2. Listen to the interview and tick the correct answers.
3. Check your answers for 45 seconds.
4. Listen to the interview for a second time.
5. Check your answers for 45 seconds. This is your final task.

1. Speaker 1
   - ☐ fears the pollution of our environment.
   - ☐ thinks that nuclear power plants are dangerous but necessary.
   - ☐ thinks that our climate is already changing.
   - ☐ is afraid of a nuclear disaster.

2. Speaker 2
   - ☐ is afraid that a war might break out because of water shortage.
   - ☐ is convinced that we do not handle our water supply reasonably.
   - ☐ thinks that hot and dry regions should not use as much water.
   - ☐ would never drink water because it is polluted.

3. Speaker 3 thinks that possible consequences of pollution can be
   - ☐ that the polar ice melts and the polar bear might die out.
   - ☐ that the climate will change and parts of the world might dry out.
   - ☐ that many low lying countries will drown in water.
   - ☐ that air pollution gets so bad that we will not be able to live on Earth.

4. Speaker 4 fears that
   - ☐ there will be a war between Asia and former Yugoslavia.
   - ☐ a nuclear war will destroy our world completely.
   - ☐ third world countries will cause a new war.
   - ☐ some of the superpowers will turn our future into a nightmare.

5. Who thinks that major problems will be caused as results of nuclear power?
   - ☐ speaker 1 and speaker 2
   - ☐ speaker 1 and speaker 4
   - ☐ speaker 2 and speaker 4
   - ☐ speaker 2 and speaker 3

5 points
(1 point each)

Gesamt-
punktezahl

Standardisierte Aufgaben zum Bereich LESEN

Testdauer:
12 min

RC 1: NY – where people from all over the world meet

Read the text about multicultural New York. There are seven gaps. Find out where the sentence parts below should go. Write the numbers in the boxes in the text. Be careful – two sentence parts do NOT fit! You should not take more than 12 minutes!

One of the reasons why New York is so interesting and fascinating is the fact that many different religions, nationalities and ethnic minorities live together. It's an extremely multicultural city and that's what characterises this place. Only think about the following figures to really realise how many different people call New York their home. There are more Italians than in Rome, more Irish than in Belfast, more Jews than in Jerusalem, more Polish than in Danzig and more Chinese than in Chinatown. It's unbelievable, isn't it? All these different people ☐ live together peacefully and make up one of the most metropolitan cities in the world. They bring in their cultures and traditions, their habits and their feasts. Just think about the many different restaurants you find in New York. Think about the different religions, festivals ☐ and the different influences you can experience. But ☐ aggression and crime can turn into a problem. In New York, for example, a person ☐ is hurt or robbed every 16 minutes. So you better watch out, especially when going by subway. Crime rates are relatively high in the subway so it's always ☐. New York has an excellent subway infrastructure and the trains are quite comfortable as they are air-conditioned. What is special about the NY subway is the fact that they offer a 24 hour service ☐. If you don't want to use public transport you can also go by taxi. There are about 11,000 caps and ☐ they stop. Whichever way you travel, New York is worth discovering anyway and you surely enjoy it!

(1) you simply wave at them and then
(2) a good thing to take nothing with you.
(3) is murdered every four hours and somebody
(4) who have got different families
(5) from different countries and even continents
(6) a good thing to keep an eye on your handbag or backbag
(7) whenever people live together very closely
(8) and festivities you can celebrate
(9) so you can go any time you want

7 points
(1 point each)

Testdauer: 10 min

RC 2: Teen problems

Match the following problem letters and the answers and fill in the numbers. Be careful – there is one extra letter that does NOT fit! You should not take more than 10 minutes!

A	My parents never allow me to go out at the weekend although most of my friends may do so. It's so frustrating to know that they can go to the cinema and I have to stay at home. I don't know why they are so strict and I really have the feeling that I miss something in life. What can I do?
B	Last Saturday my best friend asked me if I wanted to come to a party with her. I didn't know anybody there but when she told me that we would spend the evening together, I said yes. In fact she only talked with other friends and left me standing alone in a corner. Now I'm so angry and disappointed and don't want to be her friend anymore.
C	It's so embarrassing! I've got an older brother and so my parents always make me wear his old clothes. But I don't want to wear hand-me-downs all the time! All the guys in my class have cool clothes and I'm the only one who has to wear the old stuff of his brother. Is there anything I can do in a situation like that?
D	I'm such an idiot! You know, I've been in love with this cute guy from 4C for quite a while and last week I decided to ask him for a date. I suggested to go to the cinema together. In the end he only made fun of me and now all his friends laugh at me and call me silly names. I really can't stand that situation any longer!

1	That really sounds like a serious problem and the only thing I can tell you right now is to ignore that guy and to keep yourself busy with other things. Forget what happened even if it's difficult. I'm sure you are soon going to meet a really nice guy!
2	Have you ever talked with your parents about your feelings? Have you ever told what it's like for you to be a kind of outsider? What about saving your pocket money and spending it on clothes? Would that be a problem for your parents? All the best!
3	Friendship can sometimes really be a tricky thing! Ask your friend why she told lies about you and tell her that she has hurt your feelings badly. If I were you, I would also break up this friendship because bad friends are the worst thing in life!
4	I can understand you, parents can sometimes be so difficult! Try and talk with them. Ask them why you're not allowed to go out and if they don't trust you. Maybe you can come up with a compromise – going out every second weekend. I hope this will work!
5	You are right, that must have really been a hard situation for you! What about having a conversation with your friend and asking her why she had made a promise she didn't keep? Tell her how you felt that evening and that it was absolutely horrible for you. However, don't let her down for a single mistake she made!

Problem letters	A	B	C	D
Answer letters				

8 points
(2 points each)

Testdauer:
12 min

RC 3: My horror trip to Turkey

Read the text about a holiday in Turkey and then tick the sentences true, false or not in the text. You should not take more than 12 minutes!

Last summer my family and I went to Turkey. My father had booked a two week all-inclusive Club holiday and my parents and my little sister were extremely excited about going there. The only one who was not so enthusiastic was I. You know, I don't really like club holidays where you only spend your time eating, lying on overcrowded beaches and at the pool and being entertained by bad evening shows. I'm very keen on sports, being active and stuff like that. Anyway. Already the taxi ride to the airport was pure horror. My mum permanently asked my dad stupid questions like "did you turn off the light in the cellar" or "did you close the bedroom window" and my sister got sick and started to throw up. Great! I thought the holiday could only become better but in the course of the next few hours and days I should find out that this thought was completely wrong. To put it in a nutshell: our flight was delayed for three hours, the Club included everything but rooms with aircondition, there were millions of jellyfish in the sea, the buffet food was not really tasty and the evening entertainment was worse than I had expected. I cannot tell you how happy I was when I could finally fly home again. In the end, in the airplane, my little sister spilled orange juice all over her newly bought summer dress and my parents started to quarrel with each other. Believe me, it took me two weeks after our return to feel relaxed again.

(Mickey, 14 years)

1. Mickey didn't really like going to Turkey with his parents.

☐ true ☐ false ☐ not in the text

2. Mickey's parents were very relaxed on their way to the airport.

☐ true ☐ false ☐ not in the text

3. During the taxi ride Mickey's sister permanently quarrelled with Mickey.

☐ true ☐ false ☐ not in the text

4. The airplane, which took the family to Turkey, was too late.

☐ true ☐ false ☐ not in the text

5. All the rooms in the Club had air condition and were cooled.

☐ true ☐ false ☐ not in the text

6. Mickey doesn't like buffet food because he never knows what to take.

☐ true ☐ false ☐ not in the text

7. In the airplane Mickey's sister spilled apple juice over her summer dress.

☐ true ☐ false ☐ not in the text

8. Mickey's sister had bought the summer dress in Turkey.

☐ true ☐ false ☐ not in the text

9. After the Turkey holiday Mickey needed another holiday to relax again.

☐ true ☐ false ☐ not in the text

9 points
(1 point each)

Testdauer: 10 min

RC 4: Mount Everest

Read the text about mountain climbing, then do the tasks below. You should not take more than 10 minutes!

Some people say it's dangerous and stupid to do, others just think it's cool and fascinating. Personally, I don't care about other people's opinions anyway and I am simply addicted to it: climbing mountains! Why? Well, that's relatively easy to explain: it makes me feel free and independent. When I started to climb mountains I was about 22 years old and I first began with easy mountains. But the older I got, the higher and more dangerous the mountains became. Right now I train to climb Mount Everest which is the highest mountain in the world. People sometimes call it "top of the world". It's almost 9,000 meters above sea level and in earlier times it used to be considered a holy mountain. Reinhold Messner was among the first Austrians who climbed the Everest. The amazing thing is that he did that without extra oxygen. On very high mountains you have to use oxygen masks. The air up there is different to the air we breathe in every day and mountaineers need extra oxygen to make sure that their brains still work well in such great heights. You can only climb the Everest from June to September. During the other months it's much too cold and temperatures can fall down to minus 50 degrees. Climbers also need special equipment to make sure that they don't freeze to death. Many people who have already climbed Mount Everest return with frozen fingers or toes. Quite often these fingers or toes must be amputated if they don't recover again. So yes, doing a thing like that probably is dangerous but then ... no risk no fun!

Locate the text! Where would you most probably find a text like that?

1. In a magazine for outdoor and mountain sports. ☐
2. In a school magazine for teenagers. ☐
3. In the sports section of a daily newspaper. ☐
4. In a book about Mount Everest. ☐

3 points (for correct answer)

Spot the topic! What is the text above about?

1. It's about extreme sports in winter and the risks related to it. ☐
2. It's about safety instructions when climbing Mount Everest. ☐
3. It's about the fascination of climbing Mount Everest. ☐
4. It's about the fun you have when you do risky things. ☐

3 points (for correct answer)

Spot the audience! Who is that text interesting for?

1. It's interesting for sporty people who sometimes go climbing. ☐
2. It's interesting for sporty people who like to go hiking. ☐
3. It's interesting for sporty people who like watching sports on TV. ☐
4. It's interesting for sporty people who like mountain climbing. ☐

3 points (for correct answer)

Testdauer: 10 min

RC 5: The super hero that didn't have super power

Read the text about a rather unconventional superhero, then decide which of the statements below fits best. You should not take more than 10 minutes!

These days it's almost impossible to present cinema movies without superheroes. There are realistic movies on the one hand that show real-life characters fighting for others. And there are movies broadcasting fictional heroes like Superman, Spiderman and Batman who save the world. "Kick Ass" (it was shown in Austria's cinemas in spring 2010) was a movie that dealt with the superhero-topic in a completely different way. Go on and read all about it:

Dave Lizewski, the film's main character, is a rather unpopular High School student. His life is rather boring and he is mostly occupied with doing things for school and talking with his friends. One day, however, after having a rather interesting discussion about taking revenge, he orders a ridiculous green neoprene suit via the Internet, gives himself the name "Kick Ass" and starts fighting against criminals. What is different though, compared with other hero movies, is the fact that Dave doesn't have any super powers. He is neither particularly strong nor very sporty. The only power he has is that he strongly believes his pure will to help others is enough to fight criminals and villains. Unfortunately he soon has to find out that things are not that easy and he is repeatedly hurt and seriously injured. Nevertheless he becomes a hero and is finally even supported by others who help him fight for the greater good.

1. If people go to the cinema these days to watch a movie …

- **a.** they don't mind not seeing a superhero.
- **b.** they don't really know what a superhero is.
- **c.** they expect to see a superhero.

2. The most important character in "Kick Ass", Dave Lizewski, …

- **a.** leads an exciting and interesting life.
- **b.** leads a life like any conventional teenager.
- **c.** leads the life of a typical superhero.

3. Why does Dave one day decide to turn into the superhero "Kick Ass"?

- **a.** Because he felt like the world needed him.
- **b.** Because he felt inspired after a conversation with his friends.
- **c.** Because his friends told him to do so.

4. How does the figure of "Kick Ass" differ from other superhero figures?

- **a.** "Kick Ass" has less super power than other heroes.
- **b.** "Kick Ass" has as much super power as other heroes.
- **c.** "Kick Ass" has no super power at all.

5. The film "Kick Ass" has got a …

- **a.** happy ending as Dave finds others who help him with his mission.
- **b.** happy ending because Dave is no longer hurt when he fights.
- **c.** happy ending as he finds out that being a superhero isn't the right thing.

5 points
(1 point each)

Testdauer: 12 min

RC 6: The "Christmas in July" festival

Read about a special American festival, then match the sentences (1–7) with the paragraphs of the text (A–E). Be careful – there are two sentences which you DON'T use! You should not take more than 12 minutes.

A Every little child knows, Christmas is celebrated on the 24th of December. This is the case in many places in the world. But not in North Carolina in America. There people celebrate it two times a year and they have a "Christmas in July" festival. In the year 2010 it was on the 3rd of July.

B Usually the festival takes place at the beginning of July and already starts on Friday afternoon. There is a big street party, offering food and music. Americans really like going there and enjoy the different live bands playing folk and country music. They bring themselves in good mood while having a chat and eating typical regional dishes.

C The festival itself then takes place on the next day (so usually a Saturday). It starts at nine in the morning and officially ends at seven in the evening. There are more music and dance performances and people even find a dance stage where young talents present themselves and perform. It's really great watching the different shows.

D The "Christmas in July" festival is also famous for the sale of handcraft. Almost everything you can buy there is handmade and a piece of art. So walking through the festival area and looking at the different items on sale is quite nice and interesting. You can find lots of handmade jewellery and accessories like bags and hats, for example.

E North Carolina probably presents one of the best and most old-fashioned summer festivals in the south of America every year. More than 20,000 Americans visit it in one day and enjoy the tasty food, the good atmosphere, the numerous children activities and the traditional music. So don't forget to go there if ever you are in North Carolina!

(1) Selling and buying is also an important aspect of this festival.
(2) For Americans the festival is a nice way of spending time.
(3) Is live music always good music?
(4) Summing up, there's nothing better than this festival.
(5) It's the place where you can buy everything.
(6) What is it that makes North Carolina so special?
(7) What can guests expect when going to this festival?

A	B	C	D	E

5 points
(1 point each)

Testdauer:
10 min

Standardisierte Aufgaben zum Bereich LESEN

RC 7: What life is like without a job

The following text is about unemployment. There are seven gaps. Find out where the sentence parts below should go. Write the numbers in the boxes in the text. Be careful – two sentence parts do NOT fit! You should not take more than 10 minutes!

Having a job definitely belongs to the best things that can happen in your life. [ ] some years ago I was without a job for more than a year. The company where I had been working, had gone bankcrupt and so I was suddenly unemployed. [ ] But I soon found out. And the truth really hurt a lot.

Being without a job means having no money for life. If you are used to regular payment, you don't even think about certain expenses – going to the cinema or to a restaurant, for example. [ ] But if you don't get a regular salary, you suddenly start to think about everything you buy. You constantly ask yourself if you really need certain things and that simply makes you feel frustrated. Hardly anything is worse than when friends ask you to go out with them and spend a nice evening and you have to say "no" because you don't have the money for it. At times I was so angry about situations like these that I could have cried.

Another depressing aspect about being unemployed is the fact that you [ ]. At first it's quite funny to have time to watch TV, DVDs, play computer games and stuff like that but [ ]. You feel useless and start asking yourself about life's meaning and why life treats you so unfair. This makes you even more depressed and really drags you down. What is more, you write loads of [ ]. You really have the feeling that everybody is against you and that better times will never ever come again. [ ] Often they don't find another job and – because of being so desperate – start drinking too much alcohol.

Personally, I was lucky. I found a job again and I have never been unemployed since then. I'm glad that I can pay my rent and that I don't have to worry any longer if I can afford going to the movies or not.

(1) You simply do the things you want to do and that is it.
(2) Sadly, many people are not able to break out of this vicious circle.
(3) after some time this feeling really starts getting on your nerves
(4) And believe me that I know what I'm talking about because
(5) As a result people sometimes start taking drugs.
(6) sit at home all day long, not really knowing what to do
(7) Quite often companies don't even open letters of applications.
(8) letters of application and most of them are not even answered
(9) At first I didn't have the slightest idea what that would mean.

7 points
(1 point each)

Testdauer: 8 min

RC 8: Body art

Read the text, then match the headlines. Be careful – there are two headlines that do NOT fit! You should not take more than 8 minutes!

1. ______________________________

Have you ever asked yourself what body art is? Well, it's made on, with, or consisting of, the human body. The most popular forms of body art are tattoos and piercings but there are also other common types like branding, body painting or full body tattoo. People who want to change their bodies and who want to make them more beautiful have to find out for themselves what they really like best.

2. ______________________________

Body art is a phenomenon of the 20th century which has become really popular in the last few decades. It first came up in the early 1960s and since then more and more people have decided to regard their bodies as bits and pieces of art. The biggest body art exhibition took place in France in the year 1975 and part of it was to consciously provoke the audience.

3. ______________________________

Shaping is also a form of body art. As the name already indicates, it means giving special parts of your body a special shape. This is particularly important for many African or Australian native cultures and it is often seen as a symbol for or ritual of growing up. In Malakula, for example (that's a small island in the Pacific Ocean), the people have got oval-shaped heads and it's absolutely normal there.

4. ______________________________

Body art, however, has also come to signify something completely different these days. It might also mean the balance and the harmony between your body and your soul. This, too, is something that has become more important in recent years as stress and hectic pace dominate our lives.

5. ______________________________

Finally, there's not much more to say than to shortly inform about possible risks. It's clear that, whenever people change their bodies, problems might come up. They can range from skin irritation to really serious things like deformation. The only important thing about body art is that people are aware of the risks and in the end it's everbody's own decision.

(A) How did everything get started?
(B) Shaping as something illegal?
(C) An example needed?
(D) Are body art and doing sports the same?
(E) What else is there?
(F) What are we actually talking about?
(G) Taking a risk?

5 points
(1 point each)

Writing

ALLGEMEINE EINLEITUNG

Am Ende der 8. Schulstufe solltest du in der Lage sein, folgende Themenbereiche schriftlich zu bearbeiten:

- Persönliche Briefe
- Erzählungen von persönlichen Erlebnissen
- Beschreibungen von Personen, Orten und Dingen
- Texte für Schülerzeitungen
- Deine eigene Meinung zu gängigen Themen äußern

Dabei solltest du Sätze verbinden können (zB mit einfachen *sentence linkers* wie *and/but/because/so*) und eine textsortengerechte Zeitform wählen (also zB Gegenwart/Vergangenheit/Zukunft). Ebenso solltest du in der Lage sein, jeden Text logisch in Einleitung – Hauptteil – Schluss zu gliedern.

THEMENVORSCHLÄGE

Task 1:

Write a letter to one of your friends telling him/her about your Ireland holiday. Write what you do there, who is with you and what you like/don't like about the holiday. Write about 160 words.

Task 2:

Write a mystery story starting with the following words:
"I was so shocked and afraid when I came home and saw that somebody had broken into my apartment." Write about 150–160 words.

Task 3:

Imagine that there is a nice boy/girl in your neighbouring class. You would like to go to the cinema with him/her but you are afraid to ask. Now write a letter to *Dr. Flirt* asking for help. The letter should have about 100 words.

Task 4:

Imagine that Angelica from Boston is at your school at the moment. Make an interview with her for your school magazine, asking her about Boston and what she likes/doesn't like there. Don't forget to write a beginning and an end! Write about 150–160 words.

Task 5:

Write a text about the job you would like to have in the future! Which job is it? Why do you think this is an interesting job and how do you imagine your life to be in 15 years time? Write about 150 words.

Task 6:

Write a text about your personal eating habits. What do you (not) eat? How often do you eat? How important is healthy food for you? Write 160–170 words.

Writing

Task 7:

Imagine you are in Sydney, Australia, at the moment. Write an e-mail to your family telling them what you have done and have seen so far. Write 220–240 words.

Task 8:

Write a short text giving your personal opinion about the topic of piercing. Would you do it? Why/why not? Are there any dangers? Why do so many people have piercings? Write about 120 words.

Task 9:

Imagine you've got a new classmate. He is from Nigeria and all your classmates make fun of him. You now write a letter to your best friend telling him/her how unfair you think this situation is. Ask him/her what you should do. Write about 180 words.

Task 10:

Write a short summary of your favourite book. Don't forget to also give your personal opinion if you liked the book or not (and why). Write about 220 words.

Task 11:

Write a story with the following words (they don't have to come up in that order). Don't forget to give it a title. Write about 220 words.

space shuttle – astronouts – afraid – moon – earth

Task 12:

Imagine your best friend has just come back from New York. He/she now tells you all about it – what he/she liked, where he/she went, ... Write the dialogue in about 300 words.

Appendix: The final check-up

Schau dir zum Schluss die folgenden Aussagen in Ruhe an und hake ab, was du nun – am Ende der 8. Schulstufe – laut den Bildungsstandards können solltest. Aber vergiss nicht, ehrlich und kritisch mit dir selbst zu sein, und hake nichts ab, was du nicht auch wirklich beherrschst! In der dritten Spalte findest du Angaben, welche Übungen im Testbuch sich besonders auf die jeweilige Fertigkeit beziehen.

Hören			
1.	Ich kann in Gesprächen über mir bekannte Themen die wichtigsten Aspekte und Hauptthemen verstehen.	LC 3 LC 4 LC 6 LC 8	
2.	Ich kann kleine Geschichten und Erzählungen aus dem Alltag verstehen.	LC 2 LC 3	
3.	Ich kann Anweisungen, Fragen, Auskünfte und Mitteilungen im Alltag verstehen.	LC 1	
4.	Ich kann in einem Text über mir vertraute Themen die Hauptpunkte verstehen.	LC 1 LC 5 LC 6	
5.	Ich kann Interviews, Berichten und Hörspielen zu mir vertrauten Themen folgen.	LC 1 to LC 8	
6.	Ich kann Wörter, die buchstabiert werden, und Zahlen oder Mengenangaben, die diktiert werden, notieren.	LC 5 LC 6 LC 7	

Lesen			
1.	Ich kann persönliche Briefe, Karten oder E-Mails verstehen und entsprechend darauf reagieren.	RC 2	
2.	Ich kann vertrauten Alltagstexten wie Speisekarten, Schildern, Formularen und zB Filmbeschreibungen die wichtigsten Informationen entnehmen.	RC 5	
3.	Ich kann aus Zeitungsartikeln zu mir vertrauten Themen die wichtigsten Informationen entnehmen.	RC 1 RC 4	
4.	Ich kann einfache Sachtexte über Themen, die ich in der Schule kennengelernt habe, verstehen.	RC 6	
5.	Ich kann einfache alltägliche Anleitungen, Erfahrungsberichte und Vorschriften verstehen.	RC 7	
6.	Ich kann einfache literarische Texte, wie kleine Geschichten, Lieder und Gedichte, verstehen und die einzelnen Absätze inhaltlich erfassen.	RC 3 RC 8	

Appendix: The final check-up

Schreiben		
1.	Ich kann über Erlebnisse schreiben und meine Gefühle und Reaktionen auf Ereignisse wiedergeben.	
2.	Ich kann eine Beschreibung über ein tatsächliches oder erfundenes Ereignis verfassen (zB: Reisebericht).	
3.	Ich kann eine Geschichte erzählen.	
4.	Ich kann kleine zusammenhängende Texte über mich und mein Umfeld schreiben (Schule, Familie, ...).	
5.	Ich kann kurze Texte über das Leben anderer Menschen schreiben.	
6.	Ich kann ausführliche Karten, E-Mails und Briefe über Ereignisse, Gefühle und Erfahrungen schreiben.	
7.	Ich kann einfache Texte zu Bildimpulsen oder Schlüsselwörtern schreiben.	

An Gesprächen teilnehmen		
1.	Ich kann ein einfaches Gespräch zu mir vertrauten Themen führen (Familie, Freunde, Tiere, Freizeit, ...).	
2.	Ich kann Gefühle ausdrücken und auf Gefühle anderer reagieren.	
3.	Ich kann in einem Gespräch meine Meinung wiedergeben, zustimmen oder widersprechen.	
4.	Ich kann einfache Vereinbarungen treffen.	
5.	Ich kann persönliche Ansichten, Pläne und Absichten formulieren.	
6.	Ich kann Gespräche in Alltagssituation bewältigen (Restaurant, Geschäft, Schalter, ...).	
7.	Ich kann um einfache Erklärungen und Anweisungen bitten bzw. diese geben (zB: Wegerklärungen, nach der Uhrzeit fragen, ...).	

Zusammenhängend sprechen		
1.	Ich kann über eigene Erfahrungen berichten.	
2.	Ich kann Pläne, Ziele, Träume und Hoffnungen beschreiben.	
3.	Ich kann über etwas Reales oder Erfundenes erzählen.	
4.	Ich kann über Dinge des alltäglichen Lebens berichten.	
5.	Ich kann vertraute Gegenstände beschreiben.	
6.	Ich kann mich, meine Familie, Orte und Freunde beschreiben.	
7.	Ich kann meine Meinung und Pläne erklären und begründen.	

IRREGULAR VERBS, PART 2

base form	past form	past participle	
learn	learnt (learned)	learnt (learned)	*lernen*
leave	left	left	*verlassen, lassen*
let	let	let	*lassen*
lie	lay	lain	*liegen*
light	lit	lit	*anzünden, erleuchten*
lose	lost	lost	*verlieren*
make	made	made	*machen*
may/to be allowed to	–/was allowed to	–/has been allowed to	*dürfen*
mean	meant	meant	*meinen, bedeuten*
meet	met	met	*sich treffen*
must/have to	–/had to	–/have had to	*müssen*
must not/not be allowed to	–/was not allowed to	–/haven't been allowed to	*nicht dürfen*
pay	paid	paid	*(be)zahlen*
put	put	put	*setzen, legen, stellen*
read	read	read	*lesen*
ride	rode	ridden	*reiten, (mit)fahren*
ring	rang	rung	*läuten*
rise	rose	risen	*erheben, aufgehen*
run	ran	run	*laufen*
say	said	said	*sagen*
see	saw	seen	*sehen*
sell	sold	sold	*verkaufen*
send	sent	sent	*(ab)schicken*
set	set	set	*setzen, einstellen*
shake	shook	shaken	*schütteln, beben*
shine	shone	shone	*scheinen, glänzen*
shoot	shot	shot	*schießen*
show	showed	shown (showed)	*zeigen*
shut	shut	shut	*schließen*
sing	sang	sung	*singen*
sit	sat	sat	*sitzen*
sleep	slept	slept	*schlafen*
smell	smelt (smelled)	smelt (smelled)	*riechen*
speak	spoke	spoken	*sprechen*
spell	spelt	spelt	*buchstabieren*
spend	spent	spent	*verbringen, ausgeben*
spring	sprang	sprung	*springen, hüpfen*
stand	stood	stood	*stehen*
steal	stole	stolen	*stehlen*
stick	stuck	stuck	*stecken, kleben*
sting	stung	stung	*stechen*
strike	struck	struck	*schlagen*
swear	swore	sworn	*schwören*
sweat	sweat	sweat	*schwitzen*
swim	swam	swum	*schwimmen*
swing	swung	swung	*schwingen*
take	took	taken	*nehmen, bringen*
teach	taught	taught	*lehren, unterrichten*
tell	told	told	*erzählen*
think	thought	thought	*denken*
throw	threw	thrown	*werfen*
understand	understood	understood	*verstehen*
wake	woke	woken	*wecken*
wear	wore	worn	*tragen*
win	won	won	*gewinnen*
write	wrote	written	*schreiben*